Halos on Afros:
Radical Black Feminist
and Womanist Thoughts on The Divine
nikki BLAK ebonyjanice

Halos on Afros:Radical Black Feminist
Womanist Thoughts on the Divine

Copyright (c) 2016 Nikki Blak Ebony Janice

Cover Design and Illustration: Chiara Richardson
www.chiaraspeaks.com

A BLAK Bird Publishing Belle Noire Publishing Collaboration

www.nikkiblak.com
www.ebonyjanice.com

First Edition

Table Of Contents

An Introduction (of sorts)

We have scrolled and scrolled and scrolled and been unable to find the text thread that started this book. Then we scrolled and scrolled and scrolled some more and couldn't locate, amongst the 1000's of messages we send to each other throughout the week, the hilarious text thread that named this book. But if we could give you a tiny glimpse into where the idea came from, "Jesus" and "Jay Z" was a major focus of that conversation... and, "Gworrrrrrrl Let Me Tell You: From God's Mouth to Our Ears" may or may not have been one of the serious suggestions for the book title once the book was drafted. Although you deserved a book entitled, "Shake What Ya Mama Gave Ya: Twerking As a Radical Worship," we're very proud of what "Halos On Afros: Radical Black Feminist and Womanist Thoughts on the Divine" has become.

Here is a true story: This book existed for 2 full years before anyone other than the two of us said anything. The book cover existed. The final draft existed. The teachers guide that is coming with the second addition of this book existed. The cover for the second addition even existed. But completing degrees, raising babies, demanding justice from anti-black grad schools, breaking up with crazy men, falling in love, becoming even more radical, growing out our hair, cutting it off again, moving across town, moving across the country, sticking it to the man, launching other projects, growing businesses, changing our minds, changing our minds back - all of these things became a priority. So we decided to wait. Two years of "Halos on Afros" sitting on a desktop hasn't changed one thing about the way we feel about black women's voices being centered in a discussion on the divine. In fact, it has only increased our capacity for this conversation in deeper and more meaningful ways.

We hope that these essays make you think and laugh, take you higher and inspire, and that they cause you to be, even more undignified than "this." We trust that our small contribution to a discussion on the divine that is God and the divine that is Black Women will offer, just a little bit more language for what it looks like to consider black women, trust black women, listen to black women, quote black women, properly cite black women, and pay black women to teach/preach/reach.

Forever Twerking In The Pulpit,

Nikki Blak ebonyjanice

THE RIGHT RIGHTEOUS CHURCH OF SHUG AVERY

by ebonyjanice

Alice Walker is my auntie. Well - not in the sense that my grandmother gave birth to her but in the sense that she is a black woman that be out here speaking the ultimate, not going to ever take it back, truth - and that reminds me of my aunties so therefore Alice Walker is my auntie. During the month of February 2016 she was basically giving "The Color Purple" master classes and I was enrolled in "The School of Celie, Shug, Nettie, Sophia and Mary Agnes" like I was literally going to get college credit for reading her Facebook notes as soon as they were posted. Especially since, at the time, I was constructing a class with suggested reading material, objectives and learning outcomes on the topic of Womanist Theology. Alice Walker's "The Color Purple" absolutely should be required reading material for an actual academic course discussing Womanist Theology. I mean, she is credited as the originator of this word. A portion of her definition reads: Womanist: "1. Outrageous, audacious, courageous, willful behavior. 2. Also: A woman who loves other women, appreciates women's strength. Sometimes loves individual men, sexually/non-sexually. 3. Loves music, dance, herself, not a victim..." (Walker, 1984). Black women theologians, inspired by the definition and influenced by the liberation theology movement took on this "Womanist" title and began to interpret the bible in ways that included the lived experiences of Black

Women in a way that the preachment of this sacred text hadn't included them before.

I was so moved by her sharing these Facebook insights into the book that I decided to start rereading "The Color Purple." I hadn't read the book since 2005. I remember that I was reading it in 2005 because I was reading it around the same time of Hurricane Katrina and much like Katrina left New Orleans undone, I was undone as well. I mean - undone in the sense that all of my former pieces were taken apart and I was rearranged completely. How could this book hurricane and tsunami me into a new being? How could the written version of Celie and Nettie shake me any deeper than their lived characters from the movie?

Now the movie... I've seen the movie a thousand times. That's not an exaggeration either. It is a ritual. I could quote the movie from start to finish if challenged. Is there a way for me to get an Oscar for my portrayal of Mister riding that horse through the wooded area chasing Nettie as she ran screaming, "I gotta go to school. I gotta go to school?" Or for the way I randomly toss myself onto the ground in dramatic moments like Celie does when Shug gets on the train to go to Memphis and is leaving her alone with Mister after Celie has clearly fallen in love with Shug? *"Shug like honey. And now, I's just like a bee."* Or the fact that at any given moment my girlfriends and I might burst out into some random moment from the movie and no matter what we're talking about it applies. It always applies.

But this essay isn't about how much I believe any black woman of a certain age that hasn't seen The Color Purple isn't trust worthy. Or about how I once considered not dating a man because he told me he had never seen The Color Purple. Or about how no matter how many times I've watched the movie, I still cringe when Celie spits in that glass of water and then hands it to Mister's mean ole' father despite how much I feel he deserved it. This essay is about the fact that the book version of Shug Avery is an audaciously fantastical womanist character; and as much as I love the movie, rereading The Color Purple as an adult has shown me a larger Shug than the one in the movie. Remember "Movie Shug" all but begging for her father's forgiveness (For what? Being too free?), longing desperately for the approval of his God and setting herself out for the attention of men she really could do with or without?

See - we see Shug Avery show up on the scene in the movie as a mean spirited, sickly drunk woman (some say she shows up as a wicked witch and turns into Celie's fairy God mother) that has come to bring Albert the pleasure Celie just cain't give him because Celie is an ugly, inexperienced little girl and Shug is a sexy, worldly woman with experience and "It." (Gould, 2005). Whatever "It" is - Shug has "It" and Celie doesn't. Albert loves Shug and in some way Shug seems to love Albert. But that's not necessarily the Shug Avery of the book. The Shug Avery of the book is honestly neither all the way here nor all the way there about Albert. I mean, she's like - "Hey Albert boy. Hey. I see you! But ain't nobody really stuttin' you." And in the movie Shug is very preoccupied with her Father and proving to him that her lifestyle is changing. Remember when she says, *"I's married now..."* as he rides by, literally on his high horse, with his permission from Big Angry God in the sky to judge her and cast her out? Shug in the movie is thirsty for mens attention and could stand to read my book "The End of Thirstiness: Lessons on Rejecting Desperation, Being Whole, Free, Single and Satisfied." But that is not the way Book Shug behaved about her father.

Shug in the book is such a sister girl that it is her relationships with the other women characters in the book that deserves so much more attention than what the movie grants us access to. Especially Celie. To Celie, Shug is everything. She is a mother figure at points: teaching and instructing, correcting and empowering. She is a sister girl: eye rolling, teeth sucking, head rolling, "Oh no he didn't-ing and black girl instigating. And she is a homie-lover-friend. Yes. You read that right. Basically Shug and Celie are in a full blown lesbion-ic relationship in the book (which is also a conversation for another day about how Shug's freedom and fluidity in her sexuality could certainly speak to her desire/intention to be both in control of her own body and used as a tool to control others by not allowing them (or their feelings for her) to control her - specifically Albert and Celie) (Thomas, 1994). Now, of course that's not to say she didn't actually love Celie, but that's just a very brief example and point of entrance into how Shug (of the book) was such a free girl that she didn't allow the way people expected a woman to behave to dictate how she behaved or even who she loved at a time when both her culture and the dominant religion of her culture wouldn't have allowed her to be so openly sexually liberated.

Shug Avery: The Womanist Theologian

Book Shug (not to be confused with Movie Shug) is speaking to Celie about God not being an old white man with blue eyes and how she has come to know/see God.

> "Man corrupt everything, say Shug. He on your box of grits, in your head, and all over the radio. He try to make you think he everywhere. Soon as you think he everywhere, you think he God. But he ain't. Whenever you trying to pray, and man plop himself on the other end of it, tell him to git lost, say Shug. Conjure up flowers, wind, water, a big rock. But this hard work, let me tell you. He been there so long, he don't want to budge. He threaten lightening, floods and earthquakes. Us fight. I hardly pray at all. Every time I conjure up a rock, I throw it. Amen." (Walker, 1992).

See - this Shug is so free that she won't even allow herself to believe that God is the masculine, patriarchal, androcentric God that Christianity has introduced to her. She says, "Church is not the place where one finds God. Rather, one brings God into church." (Baker-Fletcher, 2002). She makes it even more clear that she is against the idea of God being a |white|man| when she tells Celie, "Ain't no way to read the Bible and not think God white. . . When I found out I thought God was white and a man, I lost interest." (Walker, 1992).

Shug was way back in 1982 (when the book was first published) preaching and teaching the good gospel of Womanist Theology and setting women free (even if they didn't know they had just been preached or prophesied to). I have a very similar testimony about unknowing and being reintroduced to God. When I got it for myself that I subconsciously related to God as a far away white man I said, "Nah. I'm cool." And I literally lost every single one of my abilities to CAN. I had to reimagine God for myself. Who is God? How do I feel about calling God "He." Where is God? How can I/do I relate to Jesus? The blonde haired, blue eyed version of Jesus vs the nappy headed, radical, revolutionary black messiah that D'Angelo preaches at the beginning of his Black Messiah album? How do I relate to divinity outside of these male centered teachings? These teachings that exclude anything that Mary or Martha might have had to say? This text that didn't give the mother of Christ an opportunity to have any say on how we come to know her first-born son? If God was to remain God for me, I was going to have to switch my church membership. I could no longer be on the role of a body of "believers" that refused to see God bigger than the human form (which is always masculine) that "He" had been forced into.

Much like Shug, "every time I found myself conjuring up God as a rock - I would throw it!" It's still a process. "He" is so ingrained in my vocabulary and my psyche as it pertains to God that sometimes I just go with it. But I'm being delivered. And now I am finding myself more and more a convert into The Church of Shug Avery (the book version not necessarily the movie version). I, too, am a teacher, sister, creative, free thinking, bold, flawed, trying, becoming evangelist, woman of a woman - out here just trying to convince my people (specifically women of color) to open their eyes, their mind and their hearts and realize that the people that control the image of God tend to use that image to control us. If we don't realize God for our own |black|female| selves then we will never see God in us and we'll keep going to a building expecting to find God instead of showing up WITH God when we arrive.

The Reluctant Feminist
by Nikki Blak

There was a time when I was extremely cautious about referring to myself as a "feminist". I was a teenager. I felt very much empowered by my mother who had raised my sister and I with no assistance from our fathers, who was outspoken and intelligent, who remained single and unattached to any man for the entirety of my childhood and did not appear to be wilting without the company or approval of a one. My mother was her own person. She still is. She is well liked and has droves of friends but is not the least bit concerned with who does and doesn't like her. She's colorful and confident. The very deliberate way in which she's gone about cultivating her own interests, living fully and simply being herself all while curating a life that she is satisfied with gave me permission to do the same.

I was confident in my abilities. I knew that I was just as intelligent as any boy my age. I knew that I was just as creative as my male counterparts, if not more so. I knew that I was interesting and funny. I knew that I was special in the same way that everyone has their specialness. I knew that I was exceptional. But I didn't think that I needed to call myself a feminist. I believed in gender roles. I believed the popular interpretations of scriptural text as expressed through the cultural filter of cis-hetero-patriarchy. I didn't know what cis-hetero-patriarchy was. I was a teenager and it was the 90's.

I didn't want to call myself a feminist. There were all sorts of negative associations with that word. I wasn't crazy. I didn't hate men. I enjoyed the company of boys. In fact, I preferred it. Looking back, I understand that my preference for associating with males was problematic mainly because it was a symptom of my overall flawed thinking in regards to gender roles and the perceived weaknesses of my sex. My preference for that which was male over female was an indication that I'd had a big ol' swig of the Kool-Aid, liberally sweetened with patriarchy and artificially colored with self hate. Somewhere along the line, even though I thought I was awesome and in spite of my mother's heroic greatness, I'd accepted the fallacy that women were somehow less than men.

This reality wasn't apparent. I didn't appear to be self loathing. However, there are always two components to any given situation: It's surface and then that which is beneath. Outwardly, for the most part, I carried myself as a feminist, even if I wasn't aware of it. I believed I deserved the same things that any man did, whether it be respect, opportunity or earnings. But I didn't want to declare that I was greater than a man. And here is where we see the same immature, confused thinking exhibited by those among us who currently complain about the straightforward assertion that "Black lives matter". Somehow, in their minds they've concluded that simply stating that something is important or great, implies a preference for it and diminishes the value of everything and everyone else. That's ignorant. No one in the history of the world has ever been offended by someone saying, "I love my mama," because, after all if so and so says they love their mama, it clearly means that you don't love your mama and furthermore, your mama stinks and ain't never done a thing right in her whole rotten life. Me being beautiful doesn't disqualify your beauty. We can both be beautiful, you know. Two things can be important at the exact same time. In fact, brace yourself -- *multiple* things can be important all at once. It's an amazing thing. Look at how you didn't spontaneously combust once that was revealed. Oh, and yes, you as a woman can be feminist and still think that men are wonderful. You as a woman can be feminist and unapologetically feminine. You as a woman can be feminist and never have the thought in your head that you're greater than a man. Identifying as feminist is not, nor has it ever been about superiority or domination. In fact, to the contrary, it is simply a philosophy and strategy that provides women with footing that is equal to men's. In case you're new to words, equal does not mean or even imply "above".

I was intelligent, but apparently not yet intelligent enough to arrive at the reality that I could be feminist and not be crazy or be fostering a superiority complex. To take it a step further, I hadn't yet become intelligent enough to even consider for a moment that the perception of feminists as man-hating loonies was the result of well crafted, consistent, persistent propaganda. I hadn't yet heard of gas lighting. I wasn't yet aware of all of the ways that women were being discredited, dismissed, silenced and made to feel stupid and insane for recognizing the workings of the cis-hetero-patriarchy agenda. I didn't know how our current system of gender based oppression enlisted women and rewarded them for spreading the gospel of sexism. I didn't know that the Salem Witch Trials were not about witches at all, but just a tidy way of excusing the torture and execution of women en masse. I didn't know I was shining my own shackles and calling them anklets. I hadn't even begun to come into my blackness, let alone my woman-ness. I didn't know that the two were already intertwined, would remain irrevocably bound and would incite each other into their current raging forest fire-like state.

There would be years of peeling back layer upon layer of myself to reveal my most vulnerable, powerful self. In all honesty, I am still peeling back layers. Each year that I live gifts me with at least one great epiphany and each thought that I have becomes more radical and leads me to one revelation after another about myself as an individual, myself within the context of society, and society as it's own separate entity apart from myself. When I turned 18, I asked my hairstylist, who I'd been going to see since I was in the 8th grade, to cut all of my hair off. It was something that I absolutely had to do and at the time, I couldn't articulate why. However, it wouldn't be too long before I realized that it was, for me, a necessary shedding. I had subconsciously decided to reject popular beauty standards and force the world to look at my prominent face. With nothing but an inch or two of hair on my head, there would literally be nothing for me to hide behind. I have a substantial forehead and a gap in my front teeth and you were about to get this work, honey. This was the first step for me in embodying an attitude that dictated that I would stop shrinking myself or modifying my behavior for the comfort and safety of others and that folk would just have to deal or avert their gaze if they didn't like what they saw.

I was rescuing myself from a paradigm in which Dinah of the Bible was at fault for her own rape. I was about to start teaching myself that instead, men should bear the burden of their own actions. I was escaping into a school of thought in which Matthew 5:29 was the gospel, not just because it was a part of what is collectively known as "The Gospel", but because it taught the good, valuable doctrine of accountability for self and respect for the boundaries of others. "If your right eye causes you to stumble, pluck it out and throw it away." Anti-Cis-hetero-patriarchy translation: If the sight of a person's body causes inappropriate sexual arousal, stop looking and don't you dare attempt to make the subject of your perverted gaze responsible for *your* thoughts, feelings or actions.

Furthermore, I was about to learn how to take care of myself. How to not make other people responsible for *my* own thoughts and emotions and by extension, my actions. No one can make me feel inferior. They can try, but my feelings are my own. What happens after that? Well, I can't be controlled. I'm in charge of me. Once that realization takes hold, you stop *reacting* to others and you learn how to respond. I became less volatile. I became more dangerous.

. . .

Presently, I am cautious about referring to myself as a "feminist". I am a grown, independent, well traveled, educated woman raising two girls of my own. I have no worries of being labeled as a "man hater", "crazy", a "bitch" or any other foolish, uninventive, derogatory term. Other people's perception of me isn't really any of my business and trust me, I pride myself on minding my own business. It is not the misconceptions that ignorant people have about what makes a person a feminist that concern me. What troubles me about the term and the movement is how closely it has courted anti-black racism.

Historically, feminism has done a poor job of recognizing the challenges that women of color face and hasn't done much in the way of acknowledging struggles that aren't universal but, instead specific to one's own race, ethnicity, and social class. Feminism has operated under the guise of ubiquitous sisterhood, therefore relegating women of color to the margins of the movement by brushing broad strokes to color us all a homogenous shade of perfectly female. Sadly, each wave of feminism has been inexplicably bound to Global White Supremacy, resulting in a legacy that has done just about as much harm as good. Further, the syntax of whiteness in third wave feminism has yielded theory and written works in which black women were cited, however their ideas were divorced from their original context in which race was a major factor.

I'm not here for it.

I'm not here to have my ideas or those of my sisters co-opted by a movement that seeks to appropriate our plight, using it to further its own agenda while leaving us to fend for ourselves. I'm not here for a movement in which whiteness is still at the centre. It is a sort of intellectual gentrification. There is nothing radical about that. At best, it is exploitive. At worst, it is violent. If I am comfortable with that, then I ought to just recline into the bosom of hetero-patriarchy and shut my mouth about oppression, which we know is something I'm never going to do. I can't. There is no point at all in me having a single subversive thought if in the end it just serves to realign me with more systems of oppression.

Granted, Feminism helped me find my feet so that I could start my journey to freedom. For that, I am forever grateful. But I needed something more. Because I am more than just a woman. My blackness is at times, overwhelming.

I need a home for all of this deep, wide identity.

For now, I believe that home can be found in Womanism. So, for now I am calling myself a Womanist. Make no mistakes, I am still learning, just as sure as I am still growing. It can all change tomorrow. Also, trust that I am not concerned at all with a specific title but rather am invested in being in community with others who seek to affirm women as well as create and maintain space for us. That is my motivation and that is my truth. My prayer is that whatever brings me closer to that truth will be what I will find and keep and that I will cast away the labels, ideas, practices, people, places, and things that don't make me who God has already declared I am.

WHAT WOULD POST MODERN HIP HOP WOMANIST JESUS DO?

by ebonyjanice

If we are the body of Christ, then Christ (in this vessel) is a Hip Hop Womanist and we gots things to discuss...

The problem with today's Christianity, in my estimation, is that it puts more emphasis on heaven than Christ. Yes - Christ as the way to heaven but not enough of bringing Christ and being Christ. You are the body, right? Then why are you so busy hoarding grace when you are supposed to be being and bringing Christ in flesh to the earth? Heaven gonna be t[here]. Isn't your job to make sure you don't arrive in heaven alone? Thinking about John B Cobb Jr's "Call Forward..." That *to actualize in this "Call" we ought to consider what is happening in our contemporary context...* (Coleman, 2008). This made me think about a brief list of systematic evils in Monica Coleman's "Making A Way Out of No Way":

- Racism
- Sexism
- Oppression
- Heterosexism
- Servanthood
- Surrogacy
- Injustice
- Rape (Coleman, 2008).

How are we addressing these things from a liberation perspective? How are we addressing these things from a postmodern womanist hip hop womanist perspective?

Sonia Sanchez says, "I had come into the city carrying life in my eyes amid rumors of death." (Coleman, 2008). A postmodern womanist theology maintains hope in the struggle to creatively and constructively respond to these realities. A postmodern womanist theology asks, "How do we "carry life in our eyes amid rumors of death?" It promotes "living in cooperation with God for the constructive social transformation of the world." (Coleman, 2008). In postmodern womanist theology, salvation is an activity. The activity of salvation, then, would include justice work, movement towards equality discipleship, the importance of quality of life, acceptance and inclusion. (Coleman, 2008).

That's because postmodern womanist theology focuses on the ministry of Jesus and the pursuit of justice as an indicator for what was (is) important to Christ. That Yeshua (jesus) would have been protesting in Ferguson and Baltimore can't be a question. It has to be the clear and obvious answer, if you've ever read the text at all. So... How are you NOT addressing these realities on a regular basis in your ministry? Why is your Sunday morning worship and your Wednesday night bible study the main focus of your weekly agenda? Aren't people hungry, homeless and oppressed due to all of the aforementioned systematic evils? According to your estimation, isn't Christ the answer to that evil? Where is Christ in all of this unrest? These are the some of the questions of a post modern womanist according to Coleman (Coleman, 2008).

I self-identify as a hip hop womanist. I know that my role as a womanist in a male dominated art form (hip hop) comes with many contradictions. But these contradictions also mirror the way it often feels to be a womanist in a male dominated religious tradition and denominations. Aisha Durham defines Hip Hop feminism as a cultural, intellectual, and political movement grounded in the situated knowledge of women of color from the post-civil rights or Hip Hop generation who recognize culture as a pivotal site for political intervention to challenge, resist, and mobilize collectives to dismantle systems of exploitation (Durham, 2007). My definition of Hip Hop womanism would add that all of these beliefs and practices are additionally grounded in spiritual knowledge as much as it is impacted by the cultural, intellectual and political.

There are obvious contradictions in considering myself a Hip Hop Womanist. How do I deal with the overt sexism, misogyny and misogynoir at work in rap lyrics and the behavior of major Hip Hop artists for years? How does a Hip Hop Womanist reconcile herself with the violence of her contemporaries? In what way can a religious leader use this secular art form in an ethical and justifiable way? Simply, my Hip Hop Womanism was raised, simultaneously in the church and "on the block." My Hip Hop Womanism causes me to quote JayZ as much as, if not more than, I quote the Apostle Paul in order to acknowledge the complexities of mine and my peers relationship with God and the Eternal. Further, my Hip Hop

Womanism causes me to call on Beyonce as a witness, as much as, if not more than, I call on Queen Esther to testify on my behalf. Womanist praxis would argue that reclaiming something for ourselves - something that has been considered wrong – and deciding that it is holy is the way that we give agency to ourselves. This is the way that we "un-other" ourselves from God and the mainstream at the same time. (ebonyjanice, 2016).

Why is your programming not intentionally culturally relevant?

Why have you found it impossible to cultivate a ministry that mirrors the way that Christ, himself, would actually deal with Homosexuality and not one rooted in fear, arrogance and hatred? Seriously... What Would Jesus Do?

Where is your actual communication around Sexual Liberation amongst black women in the church community? How long will you continue to teach abstinence and create fear and shame around the physical response and natural proclivities of the body, rather than encouraging healthy dialogue about how one might respond when these natural inclinations arise?

How long will you continue to perpetuate a patriarchal and misogynistic message within the walls of your temples? God created man in his own image, but according to your traditions - women were created a little bit less in "His" image than men; although the text doesn't support this at all.

Are you going to keep encouraging that your "boys will be boys" and teaching girls that modesty is the answer to the fact that you didn't teach your boys to respect women regardless of what they have on?

And lastly (for this list - not the entire list of questions I have in this regard), don't you see it as a part of your "call forward" to address these matters in the church? That Christ certainly would have been one of the FIRST to address these matters and not forced, dragged, (see also: begged) to engage on these topics; can't possibly be completely lost on you.

I've just been thinking a bit about my place as a hip hop womanist and how I engage the text and God's people in a way that is relevant and righteous and these are some of the issues that came up for me. How do I come "into this city with life in my eyes" amongst these realities of death? I'm thinking, very often, "What WOULD Jesus Do?" Usually, I am certain it is the opposite of the current "this."

Hoodrats in Headwraps:
Facets on Fleek
by Nikki Blak

There are these things called intersections. They are the point at which two lines cross. They exist in topography, both natural and man-made. They are present in mathematics. Today, in this conversation, intersections represent the figurative area of one's life where two identities or social constructs meet. I am black and I am woman. There, you have an intersection. I am American born of African descent. Another intersection. If I were queer and/or had a disability, those would be more intersections. We could unravel a litany of identities, social constructs and ways in which I am perceived by those who come into contact with me and create an imaginary map scarred with hundreds of hash marks, each showing places where my identities converge. I am by no means special or unique in this way. We are all a masterpiece of intersections.

There are these things known as facets. We often think of them in reference to precious gemstones. This association is especially appropriate as we discuss black women, so go ahead and imagine any gem you like. Diamonds are popular and therefore a go-to, however I'm partial to sapphires. A sapphire's hardness is only rivaled by that of a diamond, which of course is the hardest mineral on the planet. Sapphires naturally occur as result of extreme heat and pressure. They come in a vast array of shades, are magnificent in color and dazzling in transparency.

Once a gemstone is cut, depending on the angle at which you view it and the available light, the exact color and its intensity will vary. Facets are the many sides of a thing, in this particular case, a sapphire or whatever gemstone you imagined. It is the many facets of a gemstone, when viewed several at a time, that lend it it's fire, mesmerizing sparkle and beauty. A sapphire without its facets would hardly be impressive.

Let's take a little break from all of this gemology chatter so that I can share a little something with you. I admit that I'm fairly young and therefore haven't been on the Earth all that long. However, in the brief time I've been here, I've picked up a few things here and there. One of the key things that I've learned about relationships, through experience and observation is this: The quickest, most efficient way to thoroughly destroy a relationship with another human is to do one or a combination of the following things: (1) Deify them. (2) Regard them as somehow less than you.

When you deify a human being, you're robbing them of their ability to function as a flawed entity and shackling them to this false and unreachable ideal of perfection and infallibility that *you yourself* created, perhaps without any input or permission from the subject. This is not to say that we shouldn't hold each other to high standards or expect and accept mediocrity. Yes, by all means, place reasonable expectations on mature adults. However, bear in mind that no matter how brilliant, talented, accomplished or capable they are, they are still bound by the parameters that flesh, gravity and time place on them in this experience as a person on planet Earth. Positioning someone on a figurative pedestal doesn't give them any literal space or freedom. They have to be careful to maintain their equilibrium so as not to teeter off and come plummeting down. If they fall, they'll hurt themselves. Mind you, they didn't even climb up there to begin with – YOU put them there and therefore put them in danger. The act of perching someone up on the pedestal that you constructed for them doesn't even serve them and it most certainly doesn't serve you. It is also a sly, passive means of controlling them and is especially effective with women, as we often have "the need to please", thanks to society's conditioning.

In the inverse, viewing someone as less than you, is just as problematic if for no other reason than the simple fact that it is unkind. Belittling an individual is cruel, as it is a weapon formed to damage the dignity of another person. Viewing another person as less than and attempting to shame them for their perceived inadequacies says more about the individual doing the offending than the one on the receiving end. Often times, this type of mindset and behavior is a symptom of one's own feelings of inadequacy and possible low self esteem. The need to step on others to make one's self taller doesn't serve either party, as it damages the person being stepped on and creates a false sense of greatness that the offender can't maintain without the other person under them, supporting their ego.

These are the two quickest ways to thoroughly wreck a relationship. The thing that both of these practices have in common is that when put into action, they don't allow the person who is utilizing them to see all sides of their subject. If you are deifying a person, you're likely not acknowledging all of their facets. If you're viewing someone as less than you, you haven't taken into account all parts of this whole human being that according to you, sucks. You're so busy focusing on the one or two things that make them great or the areas in which they're not meeting your standards, you haven't discovered the entire breadth of this entity and you're not honoring the entirety of them on the many levels that they function and planes on which they exist.

Human beings are multifaceted. We are flesh and finite. We also have a spiritual component that is undoubtedly infinite. We're also cerebral. We're also emotionally intricate. We have pasts, a present, and a future. Since race is a social construct and many of us are quite mixed culturally, there are also the complexities and nuances that come from embodying multiple ethnic and racial identities. Some of us are gender fluid. Some of us are sexually attracted to the same gender that we identify as, or both genders, or neither. There is always a multiplicity of factors that come into play when looking at an individual's "self".

And then there are the somewhat trivial things. Did you know that it's possible for one human to enjoy many different genres of music? Yes, that's a thing! Or, hey, did you know that a woman can be a freak in the sheets and yet, still prefer to dress modestly? And vise versa. I know, it's crazy right. And interesting as well. The juxtaposition of seemingly very opposite preferences and traits in human beings makes us, dare I say, interesting. Furthermore, the complex nature of people and the way that it develops over time or changes as status and circumstances do, basically means that all bets are off in terms of being able to predict with certainty what any given person might like, dislike, or do at any given moment.

Women Are People

Did you know that women are people? That may sound like moronic question, but there's more of a problem with the fact that I have to bother to ask it than there is with the actual question itself. There's this pesky thing called objectification. You probably know what it is, but for the sake of being thorough, I'll just say that it is basically the practice of treating a person as if they were a thing or an object. It's quite common in the world, especially in terms of the perception and (mis)treatment of women. In fact, I would go so far as to say that objectification is at the center of why women are marginalized, mistreated, abused and oppressed. Female infanticide probably wouldn't be as as common a practice as it is and has been for centuries if women and girls were not viewed as objects that will likely be of no use to or burden their families, and were instead seen as actual people. People have value beyond the services they can provide and income they can generate. People are important and their lives are precious simply because they exist. So says our internal moral compass. So says God. One does not have to earn personhood. And yet, women have had to earn the right to vote via cutting up in various suffragette movements. Because, an object doesn't need to vote, right? And an object can't say, "no" to sexual advances, right? And an object doesn't deserve equal pay for the same amount of work... Because it's an object. Not an actual, autonomous person with needs, desires, preferences, opinions, and a future. An object's only value comes from how it is used. And when the object doesn't perform in the manner for which it was designed and manufactured, or it malfunctions, or it just doesn't do what you want it to do, you act out in anger toward it. You've seen people curse at their phones? Or smack their computers? Yeah, that'll teach it. And once the object's use has been expended, it's lost its beauty, or a better newer one of it's kind becomes available, the old object in question is trash.

This is literally how women are treated. Like objects, and then, like trash. It is evident in the popular reasoning that is applied in situations in which folks are supposedly asserting that women should be treated better: She's someone's daughter. She's someone's mother. She's someone's sister. She's someone's fourth cousin on their daddy's side, twice removed. She's someone's annoying, germaphobic co-worker in the cubicle across the walkway. She's someone's kind neighbor who always signs for other tenants' packages when UPS comes in the middle of the day. She's someone's *something*. She must *belong* to someone. She must perform a service for someone. She can't just be valuable by her own merit, simply because she's a human being that exists on the planet.

This, my friends, is Patriarchy hard at work. Every single human has been socially conditioned to believe that men are superior and women are inferior.

This brand of foolish reasoning further perpetuates a mindset that dictates that women are property. At best, we're merely vessels. If we're clever or cute, we get promoted to sidekick status. Failure to acknowledge our personhood allows us to buy into popular interpretation of Biblical texts that relegate very powerful women to the margins of the scriptures. Mary gets to be the mother of the Christ only because of her so-called purity. There is nothing else revealed to us about her personality that would undoubtedly set her apart from the droves of other young women of her time who had managed to maintain their virginity. We're not made privy to anything about her personality that would deem her worthy of such an incredible honor. The only thing of value she has, we're told, is her virginity. Oh, and a uterus. Mary gets to be a virgin, a uterus, a burden to Joseph, and then, Jesus' mama. That's it. In popular culture, Catholicism, and in the minds of a startling number of intelligent adults that function within the Christian paradigm, she doesn't even get to have sex at any point or become anybody else's mama. For centuries, there has been worldwide mania concerning her virginity. She's literally known as *The Virgin Mary*, which is confusing when you consider that the scriptures themselves say that Jesus had younger siblings. Mary had sex, everybody.

Let's deal with that.

Mary was a whole person. I would venture to say that there had to be a skosh more to her than her uncanny ability to keep penises out of her vagina that would make the all knowing, all powerful Creator select her from a sea of human uteruses to bear the savior of the world. I wish that we were able to get to know Mary and understand who she was, but thanks to patriarchy we've been afforded no such luxuries. While we're on the subject of Mary and her miraculous, never ending virginity, can we talk about how our centuries long obsession with it, when viewed at its most rudimentary level comes down to our preoccupation with women's bodies?

Let's talk about women as bodies. Since women don't exist in the real world as people. Let's talk about fragile masculinity, which perceives everything that is opposite of it as in opposition to it. I believe that Mary was a riotously fierce woman. I believe that Mary was a show stopper. I believe that Mary did not come to play with you heuxs, but on the contrary, she came to slay. I believe that the more dynamic a woman is, the more likely it is that she is silenced in and erased from scripture and Christian doctrine. It's the only sense that I can stitch together that would explain why such a pivotal figure – the mother of the Christ – is revered only for her body and all of the things that she didn't do with it.

The Curious Case of Mother Mary

Why is the "untainted" version of Mary idolized in Catholicism? Once again, the concept of personhood and the expectation and acceptance that a human would be multifaceted takes precedence. By refusing to accept all aspects of Mary, deifying her and placing her on a pedestal, patriarchy has destroyed the world's relationship with her. I can't learn anything of value from her, I can't build on her legacy, and I can't connect with or identify with her because there's nothing with which to do so. The only thing that the archetype of Mary teaches me is that I am my body, my body is my value and my disconnection from my own body through denial of sexual pleasure is at the center of my purpose. The grossly distorted representation of Mary teaches me that I am nothing, if not a mother. Being force fed the diet version of Mary only teaches me that my identity hinges entirely on the men in my life – a heavily encumbered, gracious husband and a brilliant, revolutionary son.

As a result, we're left to wonder, what of women that do not put their uteruses to use? What of women that do not hitch themselves to men by way of marriage? Do these women have any value? If we're relying on the presentation of Mary, the answer is a swift, firm, "No." But, we know that couldn't possibly be right, right?

I find it funny – and by "funny", I mean "tragic" that in ancient times, Hebrew society was ruled by a small number of men. I find it even funnier – and by "funnier", I mean "reprehensible" – that thousands of years later, little has changed in the landscape of our larger, Christian society. We understand that women were, at the time according to law very much viewed and treated as private property belonging to men. Of course, in our own lifetime those laws don't exist. Yet, their legacies persist.

Indeed, in the days of the Ancient Hebrews and even now in some parts of the world, there is plenty of justification for the disposal of women who do not maintain their virginity. Supposedly, this failure to remain "pure" disgraces the family from which she descends. However, there is a deeper, more political ideology at the root of so called "honor killings" and it is simply that a woman who moves through the world as a sexually and economically free being is a threat to a society that is dominated by men. The archetype of the undoubtedly iconic figure that is Mother Mary ought to cause us to question the very nature of womanhood. And yet, for many of us, the high fructose corn syrup version of Mary that we were raised on only assists us in being yielding and quiet in matters directly concerning and affecting women and furthers the interest of the status quo that seeks to keep that which is masculine at the center.

Where did Jesus get his revolutionary ways from? Are we to believe that he simply inherited every aspect of his personality and tenets of his philosophies from his Heavenly Father? Are we to believe that he wasn't influenced at all by the DNA or child rearing of Mary? If we do, then we have embraced the falsehood, once again, that she was just a vessel and in that very moment we allow the idea of woman as body to take deeper root in our personal and collective psyche. Mary has become an ancient symbol and world-wide representation of mothers. There is a litany of reasons why we refuse to see mothers as sexual beings, however, I think that for men, all of those reasons are tied to their own feelings of self worth, value, and security. The idea that a woman's personal agenda could be just as important as her duties to fulfill her obligations as nurturer and caregiver to her children, I suppose could feel threatening to a male, especially and particularly when he has been conditioned to think that he himself and his own needs and desires are at the center of a woman's world, particularly that of his mother's. There is also the ever pervasive idea that sex is dirty or shameful, even within the context of a loving, committed relationship. Therefore, if the act is dirty, then what is the person performing the act? That's right, dirty. And who wants to think of their mothers as dirty?

I think there's also something to be said of the common ways in which men have been known to treat women, especially in terms of seeking sexual gratification, and how this affects their views of the women that they allegedly love and "seek to protect", such as mothers and daughters. They are fully aware of how they've run game on women, exploited them, tossed them aside like chicken bones that have had all of the meat eaten away. If they are the least bit aware of their actions and take any time whatsoever to reflect, the realization that these behaviors are widely accepted and standard practice and that it is likely that these are the realities that their beloved mothers and daughters are enduring is somewhat horrific. Therefore, in their minds, it's easier to simply extract their own mothers from the exploitation by men equation and perch her high on a pedestal where she can remain pristine and virtuous, for all eternity. So was the fate of Mary, Jesus' mama, thanks to the guilt ridden minds of men throughout the century, whom would rather stick to the fairytale narrative of a forever virginal woman than simply treat females of the human species with a modicum of respect.

If I Am More Than a Body

If I, as a woman, am more than a body, then what is with this preoccupation with how I dress? If I, as a woman, am more than a body, then why are people who are not my hairstylist so invested in if I wear braids today, a booty grazing silky weave tomorrow, and a shiny bald head next week? If I, as a woman, am more than a body, what is the benefit of enacting legislation that denies me birth control and safe, easily accessible abortions? If I, as a woman, am more than a body, then what is so offensive about me using my parts for their intended purpose and breast feeding my infant in a public space? If I, as a woman, am more than a body, then what is at the root of the criminal justice system's apparent inability or unwillingness to convict rapists and keep them imprisoned?

It is the perception of the female as object and property that fuels outrage in response to the ways in which we choose to present ourselves and what we opt to do with our parts. It is the perception of the female as object and property that inspires apathy toward issues of women's rights and safety. It is the perception of the female as object and property that has people convinced that a revealing outfit, or a completely covered body, or the presence of her body at all is an invitation or consent. It is the perception, belief, and tradition of the female as object and property that has folk confused when they encounter an articulate woman that enjoys trap music or a woman donning a headwrap who also has had many sexual partners.

I'm here to tell you that if you haven't accepted the human female as more than a body and property, it is the will of the Lord that I puzzle you. If I haven't confused you thoroughly with my very presence, then I probably haven't done my job. I just so happened to show up in this particular body, however, if you've allowed that alone to inform your opinion of me, then you will likely never catch up. It is because there are these things called intersections. You know them as the point at which two lines cross. There are also these things known as facets. Let me introduce you to them.

I'm Gon' Let Ya Know

I officially ceased belonging to a(nother) human(s) on December 18, 1865, thanks to formal adoption of the 13th Amendment to the United States Constitution which states that "neither slavery nor involuntary servitude… shall exist within the United States". Of course, it wasn't me, myself that was freed, but my ancestors, who had up until that point been imprisoned in chattel slavery. Prior to that, the people that I would eventually descend from endured the horror of kidnapping, rape, torture, and all of the other inconveniences and annoyances that come with being enslaved for a few hundred years. After freedom finally showed up, the people that I would eventually descend from proceeded to endure yet more terrorization at the hands of white America in the form of the KKK, Jim Crow, redlining, Cointel Pro and an ever unfurling scroll of legislation that would oppress, marginalize, silence, and effectively stomp out any efforts made by black people to assimilate, educate and protect themselves, gain and amass wealth or political power, or mobilize in any way that would be beneficial to them all while the customs and norms of society reinforced white supremacy and black inferiority.

Despite social advances due to the efforts of civil rights movements, currently I myself and black women of my generation are dealing with the residual effects of the aforementioned slavery and terrorization as well as marginalization, misrepresentation, cultural appropriation, gentrification of neighborhoods that we were once corralled into and the ongoing systematic slights that are responsible for police brutality and extrajudicial killings, mass incarceration, voter suppression and lack of access to critical resources.

I am black.

I am somehow obligated to be strong. However, I must also be quiet. Not too bold. But bold enough to be recognized as black. I must be nappy, too, because that's what it is to be black. However, I shouldn't be too nappy. Actually, scratch that, I need to immediately cease with my nappiness because the general consensus is that that is not palatable. It's too abrasive. I must come across as kind. I can't complain too much. That comes across as angry. No one likes an angry person. No one wants to listen to them. I must explain myself in a calm manner. I must smooth myself out. I must if I want to be regarded as attractive. I must, if I want to be listened to. If I want to be understood. And yet, the media is constantly sending me very clear messages that I am still not very attractive. Despite my constant efforts. And the actions of the society are telling me that I'm not being heard or understood. Despite my constant efforts. Despite my moderate tone and extensive vocabulary. Despite my eloquence or excellence. By the way, I ought not be too eloquent. That ain't black, now is it?

I am a woman.

I am continually reduced to my reproductive parts. I am shamed for being a slut. I am ostracized for being a prude. Exactly what constitutes as a "slut" and what qualifies as a "prude" are not defined by me but their definitions are dictated by men and subject to change at any moment without prior notification. I am not encouraged to question this phenomenon. I am encouraged to reproduce. However, I shouldn't be too young when I do. Exactly what qualifies as "too young" is dictated by society's preferences at the time and is subject to change at any period in history. Society is code for "men". Once again, I am not encouraged to question this phenomenon. I am encouraged to reproduce. However, I shouldn't "trap a man" when I do. I am encouraged to reproduce. However, I shouldn't necessarily expect equal participation in parenting from the man with whom I reproduce. I should reproduce. But I shouldn't do it too many times. Exactly what constitutes as "too many times" is not defined by me but by society and "society", as we already know, is code for "men". I shouldn't reproduce if it's going to be a hardship. "Hardship" is code for "requiring more than minimal effort on the part of a man". However, I should most certainly never have an abortion. I am encouraged to always do what is best for my baby. However, if what is "best for my baby" poses an inconvenience to a man, makes him uncomfortable or denies him access to my body for even a short period of time, as is the case with breastfeeding, particularly in public, I shouldn't do it. I am not encouraged to question this phenomenon. I am encouraged to reproduce. However, I need to maintain my sexiness throughout the process. However, I need to remember not to be too sexy, because after all, I am somebody's mama. Which leads us back to sex. Sex is a thing I shouldn't think about, desire or enjoy. However, as a woman, I am constantly reduced to my reproductive parts. What I do with them is always everyone else's business and rarely viewed as purely my own decision.

As a member of a new, emboldened generation of black women, I'm here to announce that those days are over. The reason why is because we have collectively decided that we have endured entirely too much in the way of scrutiny, abuse and silencing to continue to be told that we are not enough or that we're doing too much. We are far too intelligent, creative, talented, beautiful and accomplished to deny our own magic, despite religious and societal rhetoric that insists otherwise. We are too wise, because we have the spirit of our mothers' mothers always with us and their memories and lived experiences hieroglyphed into our cells. We are otherworldly because we are more than just our wonderful bodies thanks to our connection to the creator and all that which is infinite. We are precious because we are alive. We are special, interesting and valuable because we are whole people. We cannot be relegated to a single body part, feature, attribute or action and we refuse to be viewed in this manner.

Do you remember the sapphire? It is the second hardest mineral on the planet, with diamonds being the first. Precious gem stones, no matter their color or lack there of, naturally occur as result of extreme heat and pressure and are dazzling in transparency. Once a gemstone is cut, depending on the angle at which you view it and the available light, the exact color and its intensity will vary. Do you remember facets? They are the many sides of a thing, in this particular case, a precious gemstone. It is the many facets of a gemstone, when viewed several at a time, that lend it it's fire, mesmerizing sparkle and beauty. I like to think of black women as sapphires. I'm certain that without the many facets that we each individually possess, we would hardly be as impressive as we are.

Beyonce, Blank Stares and Body Rolls:
Ain't I A Hip Hop Womanist Too
by ebonyjanice

I had been spending a bit of time in Monica Coleman's "Aint I A Womanist" for many reasons:

#1. The collection of writers are fantastic. The foreword was written by Layli Maparyan, a scholar/activist that wrote "The Womanist Idea" which focuses on womanist metaphysics and spiritual activism. (huge gasp) #2. Coleman's work around identifying herself and her peers as 3rd Wave Womanists is profound to me because I'm wondering where I fit in as it pertains to "waves" and in consciously identifying myself as a womanist. Where do I stand? This is a conversation for later as well. Just know that a deeper conversation on 3rd Wave Womanism will probably involve Beyonce as well some how. #3. Because Beyonce. Seriously. I have been really interested in this particular book because of Beyonce. This is the point that I will go further into in this essay.

The other day a childhood guy friend of mine posted the following on Facebook:

> Question: why do you old/young women get upset by mam or mrs/ms??? Can't even show women respect these days it seems, feel like some just want you to be like hey BITCH!!! how are you today? i prefer to use how you doing mam or yes mam

We'll get back to him in a minute but let's deal with what we're really here for first. In her initial contribution to the text, Coleman says that "Self labeling is a psychologically and politically valuable process, yet labels and identities are socially negotiated through dialogue. People may or may not agree about how to name a thing, but the process of negotiating the label is healthy and inevitable."

This certainly made me think about all of the ways that a patriarchal society insists on trying to tell a woman what to think, how to feel, what to wear and where to go. They even have the nerves to believe that they have the right to give input on whether or not her orgasm is valid and even try to dictate what she should call herself. Coleman goes on to talk a bit more about how some scholars are willing to "wrangle" over names saying that the difference between "womanist" and "feminist" is of little significance..." Many would even argue that the title "womanist" vs "feminist" is divisive and the conversation needs to be switched to "how gender oppression works in tandem with racial oppression" rather than focusing on "black women's oppression, solely." That's a conversation for another day (it might not involve Beyonce - we'll see) but I PROMISE I am coming back to this in the future (perhaps another because one day soon) because I have been explaining the importance of Womanist Theology and saving MANY men from getting slapped in comment sections, where they magically show up out of nowhere to cape for their 'privilege' and "man-splain" that they don't really "agree" with what all of the women are saying their experiences are... further proving their 'privilege" and working on getting slapped by the sisters I was trying to save them from getting slapped by.

This is where Beyonce comes in... This woman has considered herself a "feminist" for some time now. She has been very instrumental in writing almost every female empowering super hero song of our current generation: From "Independent Woman" to "Run the World (Girls)" to "Formation." But she hasn't just expressed her goals to empower women and show that they are equally capable of doing all things solely through her artistry. She has employed an all woman band for years, spoken out about issues that impact women specifically on several occasion and partners, frequently, with other women to confront gender specific conversations in relatable, revolutionary ways. And not only has she been doing activist work - she has come right out and called herself a "feminist." So why are there a group of people (many of them are so called feminists themselves) so passionate about discounting her as a "feminist?"

Alice Walker asserts that choosing the name "womanist" (for example) is connected to a sense of freedom. She writes, "I simply feel that naming our own experience after our own fashion (as well as rejecting whatever does not seem to suit it) is the least we can do - and in this society may be our only tangible sign of personal freedom."

So why can't Beyonce be a feminist? What realities have stripped her of her right to affirm for herself that she wills to be called what she wants to be called? Who gave men the right to tell her that certain things she does disqualifies her from revolutionary work (I see you Hotep Twitter) and what kind of foolywang has provoked so called "feminists" to open their SILLY mouths and say that, because of the way she dresses or because of the fact that she doesn't do interviews and protest in the ways that THEY deem "feminist-y" enough, or even because she has the nerves to be married to a man that it appears she respects... those things mean she is not a feminist? Coleman says of this kind of nit picking that:

"In order to be a feminist one must live in poverty, always critique, never marry, want to censor pornography and/or worship the Goddess. A feminist must never compromise herself, must never make concessions for money or for love, must always be devoted to the uplift of her gender, must only make an admirable and selfless livelihood, preferably working for a women's organization."

Every time I read that I giggle. But what makes me smile even bigger is when Angela Davis adds to the conversation that "such a feminist status quo, while never intended by its architects, does "establish strict rules of conduct" and serves to "incarcerate individuality."

Tell em' while I listen Angela!

Why is being able to name oneself so important? Why is this relevant at all in a space that I've set aside to talk about "womanism?" Well... because it just is. In fact, it is particularly relevant to those individuals and communities who are so often named by other people in ways which they would not name themselves. In the epic movie, "Roots," the slave master continues to say, "Tobey," while the protagonist insists his name is "Kunta Kinte." He is even willing to be whipped for his right to call himself "Kunta Kinte."

But here we are, fellow cohorts in the struggle of empowering women into the knowledge of their equal and capable space in this world and we (read y'all) have the nerves to be trying to nit and pick who gets to be a part of our squad?

Nah Cuzz."/>∗

And so as I move further into my own understanding of where I stand in this "womanist" conversation - clearly a 3rd Wave Womanist, but deeply and passionately immersed in hip hop culture in a way that makes me feel like JUST simply calling myself a "womanist" isn't enough. That I am claiming and naming myself a "Hip Hop Womanist" and willing to embrace all that might mean within the many communities represented in that one name (specifically both feminists and womanists that might challenge the androcentric, misogynistic, patriarchal, hyper-sexual and sexist reality of hip hop). I am willing to confront those realities WITH IN hip hop, as I obviously deal with them daily - but I am unwilling to take

_____

"/>∗ Cuzz is short for cousin. I know you think that the short for cousin would be cuz but some cats from the real hood told me that I've been spelling it wrong all this time. I just felt like you should know that.

off the name or allow anyone to "bully" me out of the name based on their own oppressive relationships with their own titles.

Just like Beyonce, I may be considered a contradiction within the community of people that I am obviously most passionate about serving, but that will not stop me from asserting my right and my privilege to call myself what I want to call myself. (rolls eyes) And for the men that think that our rejection of their titles means we'd rather be disrespected all together... (sucks teeth and rolls eyes) "Get a clue!" If you want to know what to call me... Just Ask!

LIBERATING ALL THE WOMEN
BEFORE AND AFTER ME:
THE TRUE MISSION OF A WOMANIST

by ebonyjanice

*"And if you think about turning back, I got the shot gun on your back." -
Erykah Badu in the voice of Harriet "Moses" Tubman*

Recently while discussing my own individual reflections on Institutional Power, I began to think through the institution of family. Below are some of the questions and answers that I believe are very appropriate for a conversation on *the true mission of a womanist* that I'm having with myself daily so I'm going to briefly share the prompts and my responses and then I'll move on swiftly to my goal of liberating all the women before and after me:

- *How is power structured within the institution?* My family runs as a hierarchy of eldership. It is largely dominated by women because my grandmother raised 6 girls by herself/after the death of my grandfather/when the 6 of them were still small children/preteens. There are many layers to this piece. We were socialized into strength/power/being in charge (as women). We were socialized into a perpetual "strong black woman" reality. We were socialized into "respect your elders," "submit to authority," "mother knows best" (and so on). This is how the hierarchy of eldership keeps its dominance. The only thing outside of submission to this hierarchy that is acceptable in the institution of our family is status in the community (status could give you more voice than your age/ position might normally allow you). Also, money could give you more power within the hierarchy of eldership - depending on how the money is distributed throughout the institution.

- Who holds positional power? Grandmother held the primary power. Then the power trickled down to each Aunt based on age from oldest to youngest (unless social status/respect from the community gave someone more power out of their level in the eldership). Then the power trickled down to the eldest grandchild down to the youngest (again, unless social status/respect from the community gave someone more power outside of their level in the eldership).

- How is interpersonal power distributed? Interpersonal power is a birthright in the institution of our family and exists in strength at whatever level in the eldership one falls. UNLESS a higher level of voice and power is TAKEN. This is what we're getting to for the purpose of this essay. Stick with me for a few more moments.

- How can individuals exercise their own personal power within the institution? If you are not at the top of the eldership and decide to do something outside of the socialized familial institutions' norms then you can exercise your own personal power within the institution by (1) Rebelling in a way that demands acceptance or (2) Rebelling and having everyone in the institution side eye you until you get back in line. Note: Rebellion of some sort is going to have to happen either way. You're going to have to boldly say, "I know that's what we've been doing/believing/having but I'm not doing/believing/having that anymore."

- What barriers exist for interpersonal and individual power? Tradition is a barrier for interpersonal and individual power. One must ask the question "What socialized agreements have we made as a family? From a small town? With obvious ties to slavery/ sharecropping and a grandmother that barely missed picking cotton? As black people in America? With deep southern roots? As Christian identifying people? As a family full of black WOMEN?" Whatever the answer is, you are going to agree with that. End of story. Religion is also a barrier for interpersonal and individual power. Do what the Bible says (solely through the accepted interpretation acknowledged by the eldership). End of story.

- What opportunities exist for interpersonal and individual power? Because we come from strength, STRENGTH IS RESPECTED. Possibly the only thing acceptable outside of conforming and agreeing with the map laid out by the hierarchy of eldership is to display great strength and clarity of purpose. If you "rebel" you better rebel with a serious purpose and your rebellion better speak to the hidden truths of the elders or prepare for that strong side eye.

Ok. Now walk with me. In my family, theoretically I fall pretty low on the hierarchy of eldership table. I am the 3rd youngest granddaughter. So that means there is 1 grandmother (now our Ancestor and guiding elder spirit), 6 daughters and 5 girl cousins higher in the hierarchy than me.

Theoretically there would only be 2 girl cousins below me in this hierarchy. That's in theory. If I had time, I'd break down how the 2 "below" me have also frequently defied the hierarchy by strength and firmness in their own truths (which often lies outside the norms that we have been socialized into in this familial institution) but I don't have time to deal with their "how" I'll only deal with my "how" (quickly) and then get to the "why!" *Why* is what we're here for.

During this journey I decided to write through the experience that lead to my first time heavy sighing and rolling my eyes at my grandmother (the top of the hierarchy of eldership) [of course behind her back and certainly not to her face because I am still living!] After I posted it on my blog, one of my elders called me so that we could discuss this post. When she first said she wanted to talk to me about it I was a little worried. I was like, "Lord have mercy. She is about to give me the business for talking about some of the antiquated ideas that her mother had." But that's not the conversation that we ended up having at all. She began to share some stories with me about things that she, too, disagreed with that she had been taught by her mother (my grandmother). She told me about how she maneuvered through those conversations as she got older and became a wife, a mother and a leader in her own community/institution of family separate from the one we shared in common. She also shared some private conversations that she and my grandmother had that also showed some of the spaces that my grandmother also (often privately, sometimes publicly) disagreed with her own teachings that had become her norms based on the way that she was raised.

That conversation enlarged me - but it also made me realize that Alice Walker's definition of "womanist" is full of so much truth as it pertains to black women and their shared (specifically familial) experiences. These shared experiences, often, due to where one lands on the hierarchy of eldership, may not even be outwardly expressed shared experiences. Meaning, we're all walking in the same tensions but haven't been transparent enough to realize.

WOMANIST Definition (Alice Walker)

1. From *womanish*. (Opp. of "girlish," i.e. frivolous, irresponsible, not serious.) A black feminist or feminist of color. From the black folk expression of mothers to female children, "you acting womanish," i.e., like a woman. Usually referring to outrageous, audacious, courageous or *willful* behavior. Wanting to know more and in greater depth than is considered "good" for one. Interested in grown up doings. Acting grown up. Being grown up. Interchangeable with another black folk expression: "You trying to be grown." Responsible. In charge. *Serious*.

Honey... I BEEN a womanist based on this part of the definition. However, I also realize I come from a family full of womanists that haven't historically had the language to name ourselves. It is my "rebellion," as it pertains to my location in the hierarchy that is forcing/has forced many of these womanist conversations to the forefront. We have been a family full of (mostly) closeted womanists; all attempting to stay "in line" while often disagreeing with the "roles" and "rules" that we had fallen into because of the "institution" when really we should have, long ago, just called a family meeting and agreed that we no longer fully agreed with those old truths. From there we could have/should have/should still rewrite what the "becoming" looks like and/or really - just come together and share our stories and give each other permission to explore what that "becoming" looks like without fear of being side eyed by the eldership (regardless of where we fall on that hierarchy). WOMANIST Definition (continued)2. *Also:* A woman who loves other women..., sometimes loves individual men, sexually and/or non sexually. Appreciates and prefers women's culture, women's emotional flexibility (values tears as natural counterbalance of laughter), and women's strength. Committed to survival and wholeness of entire people, male *and* female. Not a separatist, except periodically, for health. Traditionally capable, as in: "Mama, I'm walking to Canada and I'm taking you and a bunch of other slaves with me." Reply: "It wouldn't be the first time."

This part of the definition further defines my experiences and the womanist experiences of pretty much all of the women in my family. Specifically I want to deal with the last piece: "Mama, I'm walking to Canada and I'm taking you and a bunch of other slaves with me." Reply: "It wouldn't be the first time."

Kelly Brown Douglas says of that response from the mother that, *"One of the attractive features of Walker's definition is an intergenerational dialogue between a mother and daughter. A young girl tells her mother about her plan to gain freedom. The mother informs the girl that she would not be the first one to carry out such a plan. The mother connects the young girl to her past. She provides her with an opportunity to learn from and become empowered by the freedom struggles of her foremothers."*

That's what has happened in my life as someone in my family that has slightly rebelled and refused the wholeness of the agreements formed by the hierarchy of eldership. I have constantly told my grandmother, my aunts and my own mother that I am going to "walk to Canada and am taking a bunch of slaves with me" and consistently after *I assert myself boldly (contrary to the rules/roles established by the eldership), it is THEN that I learn that I wasn't the first (nor will I be the last) to walk in this direction towards becoming a whole, free woman.

Here's the issue: As we continue to dive deeper into our understanding of a womanist theology, a theology that empowers us as |black|women| to assert ourselves, rightfully, into the conversation of God, it is equally important for us to engage in these conversations with the elders (regardless of where in the hierarchy we are normally positioned) and vice versa, by having these conversations with those that are coming after us. This idea that this "walk to freedom" has been an intergenerational walk that I've only learned as a result of my "rebellion" from my position in the established hierarchy is mind boggling. The work of a womanist is to push the next generation closer and closer, further and further, deeper and deeper into the divine truths of liberation. There should be no secret amongst the women in our families or our communities as it pertains to our socialized institutions of hierarchy. We all needed to know the stories of the womanists before us so that we wouldn't have spent so much time (for those of us that did) trying to please the eldership when really the eldership (often secretly) wanted us to go deeper, higher and further than they were able to into the direction of wholeness and self-actualization.

So, that's where the true mission of the womanist comes in. We are on a mission to make sure that we're not just studying, learning for ourselves and then simply writing about these truths - but that we are also using our own familial institutions to bring our sisters, cousins, aunts and even our mothers and grandmothers out of "Free Girl Hiding" into the light of freedom and truth seeking and telling. Harriet Tubman threatened to shoot and kill anyone that set out with her towards freedom that wanted to turn back. Her mindset was that, if you leave with us and then decide to go back, you make it even more likely that those of us heading forward will be captured and THAT is not acceptable. So "if you think about turning back, I got the shot gun on your back." That's where I am now in this journey of freedom. We are going to be free over here. And I'm going to tell it and talk about it boldly so that those behind me in the coming generation of free girls in my family don't have to feel like they have to "rebel" in order to assert themselves boldly in this hierarchy of eldership. That Ciani, Ari, and Marlee will never have to "happen" upon the truth of their womanism is the mission. But also, that those higher than me in the hierarchy of eldership will feel more compelled to come "out the closet" and tell the stories of their own personal journey towards wholeness, self-actualization and freedom. That is my ultimate mission on this womanist walk daily.

Parade of Pink Dresses
by Nikki Blak

In the spring of 2016, my 2-year-old daughter declared that she didn't want to wear anything that wasn't pink and wasn't a dress. Pink dresses, only. I had seen it coming, because well, I had already become well acquainted with this particular human, so I wasn't entirely caught off guard when it happened. The foreshadowing had occurred in the fall of the previous year, when frustrated by her daily rejection of every single stinkin' adorable romper, pair of shorts and pants that I tried to wrestle her into all summer long, I hopped online, bought her 12 dresses and accepted defeat.

What I didn't anticipate was her rejection of every dress that happened to not be pink or at least a shade of berry, which was 3 out of the entire dozen. Because pink isn't my jam. Actually, it isn't that I have anything against pink. It's just that I'm a lover of color. So, I don't *think* about pink. I just pick the garment in the color that's most appealing to me at the moment or in the shade that looks the best in that particular cut and style. As a side note, if given the option, I almost never select or wear black.

Because, color. And black isn't a color.

So here we were in the midst of winter, with the wardrobe budget for the season depleted and only 3 pink dresses to rotate until spring brought warm weather and the justification of new apparel purchases. As spring approached I got so accustomed to putting her in those same pink dresses and enjoying hassle free mornings in which my toddler didn't literally run away from me as I was trying to dress her, I sort of forgot that she had preferences. Well, maybe I didn't forget. I guess I just became hopeful that she had gotten her fill of pink dresses and that come spring, we could move on and have glorious romper and shorts moments in all of the glorious hues. I started buying warm weather garments here and there... And hardly any of them were pink or dresses. By the time May rolled around, we were back to our difficult mornings full of disagreements about what would and would not be worn. After several weeks of the foolery, I had a come to Jesus with myself in which I realized and accepted that my daughter just wasn't going to be happy in anything that wasn't pink and wasn't a dress.

Thus began the Parade of Pink Dresses. I mentioned on social media that Rosie will only wear pink dresses, now and I guess I'd better get myself together. And by "get myself together", I meant "stop holding my breath in anticipation that she would wear that one adorable blue romper or that too cute, green striped boat neck three quarter sleeved blouse and orange skinny jeans combo, purge her summer wardrobe of pretty much everything that wasn't pink and wasn't a dress and buy all the pink dresses I could find, by any means necessary". My friends turned up about it and rallied in support of The Parade of Pink Dresses. By the end of that week, we were getting toddler sized pink dresses in the mail from folks who love us and who we love right back. Friends were wearing their pink dresses in solidarity. People were asking me what size she wears and texting and emailing photos of pink dresses for our approval. It became a thing. It was sweet and entertaining and fun and just more proof that we are so blessed to get to be a part of an amazing community that will protect, provide for and celebrate its precious members. I am so grateful.

Several weeks after the Parade of Pink began its procession, a friend messaged me on social media with some more pink dress options. We chatted briefly about sizing and what Rosie would and wouldn't like and in the middle of it she said, "You're a model parent," which I took to be slightly sarcastic, not in a malicious way, but meant jokingly. We're a hilarious, smart-mouthed tribe of dry tones and side eye. I responded with a laugh and followed with, "I just don't want to waste my money on clothes that I personally love and she can't be bothered to even consider wearing," to which my friend replied, "But I mean, to let her have agency… like her choices are valuable choices."

Oh, major key… I hear you.

I've been told many a time in my short life that common sense ain't always common. That is to say that things that are natural for *you* and things that just make sense to *you* are not necessarily natural or sense making to all. That which is obvious to you is a daggone mystery to others. And then there are times when you're doing something for one reason – a reason that you assume to be the most logical reason – but that reason isn't even the reason you're doing it. Or it's revealed to you that there is a greater reason. For example, here I am allowing the Parade of Pink Dresses to march up and through my house and down these here streets because I simply don't have the energy to argue with a toddler over something as insignificant as a style of clothing and a color. Can she still do the toddler things in a dress? Yes. Is she still appropriately dressed for whatever it is we're doing? Yes. Is she clothed? Yes. Well then, seems like a non-issue to me. However, what someone else extracts from my willingness to consider my child's clothing preferences is respect of autonomy, honoring her choices and empowerment. And what I realized when she said that was that yes, that's exactly what I was doing, even when I myself wasn't paying attention to it.

What I believe about parenting is that in this human experience on this Earth, we are entrusted with nurturing and guiding the souls that come through us, be it by birth, circumstance, or adoption. Children are a gift from the Creator. They are a reward. They are not a right. They are a physical manifestation of God, just like you and I are. They are not property. They are not mine to do with what I please. They are whole, autonomous people with their own callings to heed and paths to tread. Rosie is not Nikki-the-sequel. She is not my opportunity to realize a personal dream or fulfill an aspiration. Hopefully I got to live my own life. If I didn't, too bad, so sad – her life is her own and shame on me if I don't allow her to live it and enjoy it on her own terms. In fact, if I didn't get to be as free and black and nappy as I had hoped, if I was discouraged, stifled and sabotaged, that serves as even more of a reason for me to do everything in my power to ensure that my child have the opportunity to be herself and live the full breadth and width of her magnificent life, liberated, empowered and therefore able to empower others.

Basically, I want my black girls to know their magic.

I have a 16-year-old. She is the youngest of my sister's children and I have raised her from the age of 3. When she was 7-years-old, tired of dealing with episodes of whining and flinching when dealing with her tender head, I suggested we loc her hair. She confidently said, "Yes," and committed to the regimen of grooming her head full of shoulder length kinks into a gorgeous forest of coils that then locked and grew down her back. She wore them for about 5 years, head held high the entire time. Sure, she was a part of a community in which locs and other natural hairstyles were standard issue, even expected. However, in her school, amongst her own peers and even in her immediate family, she was always the only one with such a "daring" hairstyle. That's challenging – to be the only one. I'm sure she had to navigate her way around a profusion of micro-aggressions, ignore some of the most ignorant comments and field her fair share of foolish questions and back handed compliments. As competent adults, it can be an intimidating situation, so just imagine the strength and grace that it a child must command to withstand attacks from peers about one of the things that they're likely the most sensitive about – their appearance. Yet, she was not deterred from wearing her hair the way she chose. I have a brave girl.

Once their time had run their course and she was ready to move on to something new – translation: study hours upon hours of YouTube tutorials and experiment with her hair like a typical teenager – I spent 7 days over the course of a summer, picking her locs out, one by one, for 8 hours a day. Once every single strand on her hair was loose, I shampooed, deep conditioned, blow dried, pressed and trimmed her hair. It was all on the strict condition that she would never chemically relax and therefore damage her hair.

I'm a hairstylist by trade, licensed in the state of California. During my career, I'd serviced a clientele that was mostly black and mostly female and I watched them struggle with the hair issues that we as black women often have. In a few special cases I was able to help them navigate their way through appearance insecurities that manifest themselves in preoccupation with hair – it's length and texture. It is a pathology that is borne of racism, enculturation, colorism, and the desire to assimilate into a culture that oppresses that which is "other" and shames attributes that do not resemble or conform to that which is accepted as "normal", deemed valuable or regarded as attractive. Black women know that chemical relaxers have the ability to literally dissolve the hair our heads and eat through our scalps, and yet, we've got to have them. Because, beauty standards.

I didn't want this for my girl. I wanted health, freedom, and a chemical burn free scalp for my child. I wanted my black girl to step out into a light drizzle without a single thought of her hair. I wanted her to jump into a pool, unencumbered by fear of what her hair might do. I wanted her to enjoy a work out regimen that involved sweat and hair washing without the inconvenience of having to "deal with" her hair afterward. Shackled to some style that has been deemed appropriate and pretty by folk you don't even care about is no way to live.

I wanted freedom for my girl. And I had an idea of what that might possibly look like because I was free, or at least trying to get that way.

I would call myself growing my hair out (to be worn nappy, of course), only to turn around and shave it all off 5 minutes later. Because ain't nobody got time to be shackled to some hair. I got things to do. My clients would marvel at my lack of detachment to the dead follicles coming out of my scalp. And I'd always say, "It's just some hair. It'll grow back. That's it's job. That's all it does. Grow back."

I'm not these things that someone told me was important. In fact, the person(s) that told me that this random assortment of things and stuff – hair, whether or not I have a man, a particular kind of job or a job at all -- was important didn't even invent that idea. Someone told them. And someone before that someone told them. And without proof, they each fell in line and believed it. It's a lie.

I am beautiful and valuable, simply by virtue of the fact that I exist, created in God's image. So are you. Because God said so. And that's the final word.

Most of the time, I'm out in this world, feeling like Sethe. I can't see my children kept from their freedom the way that I was -- the way that we all were at some point. There's no telling what I might do if the feeling even rises up in my spirit that my children could be stifled or enslaved.

I'd also better make sure that I'm not the one binding them up. I'd better make sure that I'm making way for the Parade of Pink Dresses. Because today's wardrobe preferences and the bravery and language to communicate them will surely become tomorrow's assertive, "No," in response to an unwanted sexual advance. Today's avante garde hairstyle may become the nerve built up to find an intact glass ceiling and bust it wide open. Today's difficult attitude may become tomorrow's audacity to challenge an unjust system. Today's mess is tomorrow's art. Today's empowered little black girl is the magic that we're all in need of.

Thoughts on Thots
by Nikki Blak

I'm convinced that there is some sort of cisheteropatriarchy handbook that is in circulation, composed at the dawn of time and passed down from generation to generation, the contents of it's pages reserved for the consumption and comprehension of the cis gender male mind, only. Some cynics will say that this handbook is the Bible. Though I will not for a second hesitate to agree that many of the passages, inferences, and interpretation of scriptural text are beyond problematic, it is not the sexist play book that I speak of. The one that I imagine is a quicker read with fewer pages, doesn't have a discernible storyline, is free of characters and may even boast a few illustrations. Actually, maybe it's more a reference guide and not necessarily meant to be read from cover to cover in order, but has tabs that lead you directly to where you need to go.

Perhaps, if a woman rejects your advances while you're on street harassment duty, you whip out your handy dandy Cisheteropatriarchy Reference Guide, locate the tab that says, "Rejection Responses", flip to the page and run your finger down the bullet points until you get to one you want to use. Ahhhhh, yes. This looks like a good one. "Ugly hoe!" you shout in her direction as she continues to ignore you. Then you congratulate yourself for a job well done.

The ancient Cisheteropatriarchy Reference Guide offers quick tips on mansplaining and impressive displays of toxic masculinity and gives step by step instructions on how to effectively Gaslight, avoid emotional labor in close relationships with females of the species and how to shirk responsibility for everything including but not limited to one's own behavior to child care and rearing.

In my mind, cis gender men sign the inside cover of each other's like high school kids do with their yearbooks in the days before summer break. They scribble cute little notes that say things like, "Don't ever change, bro," and "Keep in touch," followed by their contact information. The seasoned CRG owners have its passages memorized. Fathers pass their own weathered and worn copies down to their sons like family names and genetic traits. Everyone who has been issued a copy is sworn to secrecy and the spine of each book is equipped with an explosive device that allows it to self destruct if ever it is discovered by a woman.

How else does one explain the seemingly well rehearsed, standard responses from so many cis gendered, heterosexual men when challenged in even the slightest way by that which is feminine? I've witnessed so much identical behavior and have been called the same vulgar and unimaginative names by a vast variety of men over the decades, with such predictability that I could set my watch by it. Everything from the weak pick up lines and wilted bouquets of disingenuous flattery issued with the expectation of praise to the backhanded compliments to the verbal threats of physical violence are replicas of each one that preceded it, with it's only difference being the mouth from which it cracked. There is clearly a book they're all reading. I'm sure of it.

Every single predatory act is standard issue and lackluster. From the supposedly "great writer", William S. Burroughs who publicly murdered his wife in cold blood, to Miles Davis, who regularly beat the women he purportedly loved into oblivion, to Abraham of the Bible who married his sister and then pimped her out to the Egyptians to save his own life. It seems that throughout the centuries, the tenets and practices outlined in the Cisheteropatriarchy Reference Guide are rigorously upheld and hardly ever improved upon or updated. Rarely, if ever is a new tactic introduced. What's more, the men who execute the moves encapsulated within the pages of the CRG with adept precision are excused of their conduct and revered by their culture.

On Name Calling

There is most certainly a book. It gives the cisgender, heterosexual men the guidelines that will, if followed closely, assist them in showing up on the planet as the worst possible version of themselves. It's helpful in that way, if you're into that sort of thing. From the looks of it, droves of cisgender heterosexual men are definitely into that sort of thing.

According to a 2014 study conducted by the organization Stop Street Harassment, of the 2,000 individuals polled nationally, 65% of the women had experienced street harassment, 23% had been sexually touched, 20% had been followed, and 9% had been forced into a sexual act.

I personally have experienced street harassment on an almost daily basis since about the age of 12. All of the women that I am friends with that are in my age group have experienced street harassment. I have a few friends who have been touched and some have been followed, myself included. And of course, when we are unresponsive to the unsolicited attention, or even worse, verbalize our lack of interest, disapproval, or express annoyance, we are met with an onslaught of verbal abuse and in some cases, threats of physical violence. It is a phenomenon so common that we've become conditioned to expect this display of toxic masculinity.

It has been my experience that when a person resorts to name calling, it is often a manifestation of how they feel about themselves. Name calling is an act of violence. A person may not be able to carry out physical acts of violence for reasons ranging from not having yet built up the nerve to do it, fearing the consequences that they may face if they do it or just simply being physically unable to. However, as was stated in Pulitzer Prize winning reporter, Amy Ellis Nutt's Washington Post article about the Orlando nightclub shooting in June of 2016, feelings of self loathing often drives humans to assert their dominance over others as a way of reconciling negative emotions. We see this frequently in men and it is a manifestation of toxic masculinity, which is "a specific model of manhood geared towards dominance and control," according to writer Amanda Marcotte. She goes on to express that toxic masculinity is fueled by "persistent pressure to constantly be proving manhood and warding off anything considered feminine or emasculating".

When a woman, who is traditionally viewed by most modern societies to be less than a man says, "No," to a man in actions or words, it is emasculating. Why is that? Because men are constantly being told through media, customs, religion and every single thing that informs their perception of themselves and the world that they ought to be in control in every scenario and circumstance and furthermore, since women are less than they are, they are being robbed of an inherent right to assert their own greatness and dominate. Consciously, they recognize this as being belittled. However, the truth is that no one can *make* another person feel small and so if that is the feeling that someone is experiencing in a situation, they likely stepped on the scene feeling that way. Typically, when women stand up, men who have rooted their masculinity in the ability to dominate, find themselves shrinking and in an effort to mitigate those feelings of insecurity, attempt to expand themselves or take up more space by becoming violent, in words, deeds, or a combination of both. In these instances, "Bitch" is actually shorthand for, "I feel invisible. I'm out of control. I'm lost. The identity that I've invented for myself is informed by false representations of masculinity."

The Language of Invisibility

We are always inventing something, especially when it comes to the ways in which our communication is most evident, language. And by "we", I mean black folk. Our talent for repurposing, modifying and playing with language is one of the things that, as a writer, I often find most endearing about us. We are quick to omit or add a letter to a word or add or omit a word from a phrase. It is this linguistic magicianship that often influences the most current slang and inevitably, our vernacular is adopted by the larger society and finds it's way into the mainstream. We did it with phrases like "in the cut", "turn up", "chill out" and "wild out" and words such as "fresh", "dope", "holla", "hyphy", "shawty", "swag", and "bae". You cannot go anywhere without hearing black Americans' influence on English.

Name calling often makes appearances in slang invention and usage. Names can have positive or negative associations and connotations, or even be a mixture of both. For every term of endearment such as "boo", "son", "shawty" and the every popular "bae", there is it's negative, counterpart like "jive turkey", "sucka", "ain't shit", "bitch made" and "ho". One of the newest editions to the slang book roll call is "THOT".

What is a THOT? It is an acronym for "that ho out there", "that ho over there", "thirsty hoes out there" or any other variation of insult directed at women that can fit within the 4-words-each-of-which-must-start-with-T-H-O-and-T parameters. The word has hip-hop origins and according to rappers, describes women that are sexually uninhibited, initiate and are eager to engage in sexually risqué practices, and are, for a lack of a better word "hoes". Well, why not just call these women "hoes"? At first glance, THOT might look like a synonym for the classic default term to describe a sexually permissive woman -- "slut". However, upon closer inspection it has become apparent that being a THOT is not entirely about promiscuity. The word smacks of classism and by extension, carries strong racial overtones, since we know that race and class are more often than not bound together. Typically, in it's early days, the word THOT described a hoe that was at best "basic" and lacking style and good taste and at worst, impoverished. Of course, if she's poor she's not able to afford the things that would increase her value (because, women have no inherent value, all on their own, simply by virtue of the fact that they are human), such as exclusive, high end designer apparel, expensive tastefully furnished and well cared for homes in "good" neighborhoods, luxury cars, the latest technology and access to fine cuisine and a social circle occupied by the wealthy and well known. Overtime, it has gone the way of "bitch" and "hoe" and simply become a catch all phrase for women who displease men in any way.

The addition of THOT to the arsenal of verbal weapons that men (and some women) use to cut down women and communicate a desire to be violent is just a part of the vocabulary that comprises a language of invisibility. Though modern philosopher Immanuel Kant asserted that language originates in logical thought, there are those that believe that to the contrary, language is a representation of emotions and experience. When it comes to slang and negative labeling in particular, I do agree that the complex system of communication known as language is indeed powered by feeling. There is no logic present when feelings of jealousy, superiority, entitlement and rage arise. Inventions of negative labels such as "THOT" convey an inability to wrangle and subdue feelings of anger and one's own personal thoughts of insignificance. If a person's value is bound to their ability to own or control someone else, then it is inevitable that they will more often than not end up feeling value-less. Why? Because it is not the nature of humans to be controlled.

The term "toxic masculinity" initially made it's appearance in the mid 1990's and contrary to what you might think, does not find it's origins in modern feminist theory. It is a term coined by Social Psychologist Frank S. Pittsman and Mythopoetic Men's Movement founder, Shepard Bliss to explain the scourge of hyper masculinity that has been and continues to be physically, emotionally, mentally, and spiritually destructive, not just to the women who must endure it's violence but to the men who demonstrate it. It is suggested that toxic masculinity is the result of paternal absence. It is a theory that may have sturdy legs when you consider all of the ways in which absence can manifest. It may not be the literal absence of a father which sets the scene for displaced masculinity, but the absence of positive male voices and representations in all aspects of society and culture that would allow boys to witness celebrations of diverse, nuanced actualities of the male experience that is not corrupted by the insatiable hunger for power and strength that is at all times unyielding.

My thoughts on the word THOT and all of the other ugly monikers like it that persist in our culture, rife with cisheteropatriarchy are that, these negative terms and their themes are not ours to own. They do not belong to women. We didn't create the stories attached to them. We do not embody their essence. Nothing that we do or say make them true. The word THOT is a lie manufactured by a masculinity that is virulent and fragile. It is the bedtime story spun to sooth the ego. It is the poisonous cake, men have been coaxed to eat to make them grow large in a wonderland in which women are their equals and they just can't seem to navigate their way through.

IT GOES DOWN IN THE COMMENTS:
A POST MODERN HIP HOP WOMANIST VISION
OF SISTERHOOD THEN AND NOW
by ebonyjanice

Some days I sing a song called, "Don't read the comment section." It goes like this:

(to the tune of Pop Goes the Weasel)
"Don't read the comment section.

Don't read the comments.

If you read the comment section.

You will soon regret it.

Penny for the thoughts in your head.

Penny for your ego.

That's far more than comments will pay.

STOP! Why'd you read them?"

Ok. I've never sang that song. I just made that up. But seriously... on a regular basis I find myself eye rolling and heavy sighing for extended periods of time beyond reading an article or a blog post, having scrolled down and accidentally given the comment section any of my energy.

For example; I remember when Ayesha Curry tweeted that she likes to "Keep the goods covered up for the one who matters" in regards to the "latest fashion trends." I know - that was a good little while ago, but to date there are still people on social media that use Ayesha's comments as a way to shame women into wearing what they want them to wear or behaving the way they want them to behave. I genuinely believe that Ayesha's comments weren't intended to be harmful but they are very problematic in that they spark these kinds of debates about the ways that women dress and the reactions that they get from (often unwanted) attention as a result of their clothing. The comment section of blog posts about these series of tweets were horrendous. Men were in those comments big upping Steph Curry for marrying a woman that "cooks, is beautiful and knows her place" (insert hard blinks and eye rolls here) while tearing down women that don't dress, act or think like Ayesha and deeming them hoes and unworthy of basic respect, commitment and love.

Note: Just in case you didn't know, those short shorts and that halter top makes you a hoe. Despite the fact that you have possibly been celibate for five years and 2.5 months. YOU IS A HOE!

But the men aren't the main ones in the comment section that make me want to scream. It's usually, most often the women that have me riiiiight on the verge of pulling my hair out. I've seen women say things in the comment sections of tweets, articles and blog posts about the Ayesha Curry tweets agreeing that women are responsible for the way that men treat them and view them based on the way that they dress. I once saw a woman in a comment section giving a detailed account of how, "women that dress like xyz and get raped are essentially asking for it." Yup! In real life. A woman. A real life woman said this. These are generally ideas that you would imagine are solely held by menfolk that haven't checked their idiotic ideas about women's bodies at the door. These men believe that women's bodies were made for their consumption and that's it. So it's no surprise that these men would believe that the clothes that a woman wears is a reflection of her desire for his attention. He can't fathom that she got dressed this morning not thinking about him at all; that she simply wore that skirt because she likes the fabric, fit and the way it forms her curves just right... NOT for his pleasure, but for her own enjoyment.

When I see a woman sharing these same unfortunate, sexist ideas I am convinced that she is trapped in a time portal; that the time space continuum broke and that the gamma rays burst through and transformed her mind into mush. Extreme and super dramatic description but in real life son... Really? Additionally, I am concerned that if she believes that the way she dresses is a request for attention, then how little value has she placed on all of the other things that should be considered of value BEFORE her appearance. In her mind, her body is a party and she is perpetually ready to get it started!

This essay isn't really about Ayesha Curry though. I actually like her. I appreciate that she is a young, beautiful, seemingly intelligent woman, wife and mother - that hasn't allowed the fact that she is married to a ball player to cause her to become a quiet, voiceless version of the opinionated woman that she clearly is. While I don't agree with some of the things that she has said, I think her reality stems from the conversation I'm actually here to touch on a bit: Sisterhood. Yup! I'm here to deal with the way Sarai threw Hagar under the bus in an instance when her own voice (probably not but maybe) could have made a major difference for the questionable future she would soon live out with the F*ck Boy formerly known as Abram.

So we know this story. Sarai wants to give Abram a baby. Sarai is barren. She offers her Egyptian slave, Hagar, as a concubine for Abram. I can't even deal with the emotions of my extremely tardy revelation of all the rapity rape throughout the Bible (specifically as it pertains to Hagar) but read Sisters in the Wilderness by Delores Williams when you get time. So then when Hagar becomes pregnant Sarai instantly realizes that this was a terrible idea. After the baby is born she begins to treat Hagar very harshly. We know it must have been harsh because Hagar was willing to (1) take her baby and (2) run off into the wilderness with no protection and no covering. As Hagar was a slave, we also can envision the harsh treatment she must have been receiving from Sarai as so extreme that she was willing to literally put her life on the line as a runaway to be out of the way of Sarai's control and mistreatment.

All of this reminds me of WGN's "Underground," a show about slaves that decide to run away from their plantation, risking it all to choose freedom, no matter how dangerous the unknown world outside of the plantation they are fleeing from may be. The plantation owner, Tom, is in a full blown relationship with Ernestine, a strong willed slave woman doing what she has to do to keep her three children (presumably Tom's children) as safe as they can be - on a plantation. The owner's wife Suzanna knows that Tom ain't no kind of good and is in love with Ernestine, but does she raise up on Tom, put him in his place, and remind him that the only reason he is in possession of this plantation is because he inherited it the "good ole' boy" way by marrying into her family and receiving it as a gift since Suzanna, a measly ole woman, couldn't inherit it on her own? Nope! Suzanna decides to treat Ernestine like she is a trifling-gutter-butt-trollop that is putting some kind of wicked witchcraft spell on her simple-minded husband and causing him to want her instead of wanting Suzanna.

Dear Suzanna, You do realize that I am a slave, right? You do realize that I am your husband's property? Right? You do know that because of my current position as property, I do not even have the ability to give consent. You do get that right? You do see that I am being raped, right? You have imagined that if I could have my own man, I would be with him and not with your ole nasty tail husband, don't you?

Oh.

You can't see that?

Because you're too blinded by these antiquated ideas of southern-ness, woman-ness and your precious white-ness and would rather play the victim than to join forces with me to teach Tom the lessons of "Faithfulness" and "Loyalty."

But nah.

*You aint sh*t and yo man ain't neither.Sincerely,Ernestine*That's the letter I wish Hagar would have written to Sarai too. And further, that's the letter that I'm writing to my sisters that stay in the comment section dogging other women out and erring on the side of idiocy by agreeing with the misogynistic, sexist and rooted in racist ideas that (black) women are less than and should present themselves in a certain meek, feeble light in order to be considered worthy. On top of that, the realities for black women are even harsher, in that we have been forced into certain roles in a postbellum America that, in an effort to "feminize" ourselves - having spent so many years working as hard as our men in the fields - we often land at extremes in our portrayal of our own selves; and in the eyes of others. Either we became the super saved, "Holiness is right" completely covered up mother on the Mother's Board or we became the bump and grind, twerk captain, overly sexualized by the men that claimed they would love and protect us by any means necessary. (For Example: Why are the women in that Cash Money's video for "Oh Yeah" wearing string bikinis and the men are wearing fur coats... on an iceberg! THEY HAVE ON STRING BIKINIS ON AN ICEBERG!)

I digress.

Here's my overall thought:

"Patriarchy is Poop." - Rosie Sandbloom, age 2Patriarchy sucks. It is a thing that has existed for a very long time! It sucks and I wish it would stop. Sarai and Hagar were both victims of Patriarchy Poop! True enough.

But Sarai really played Hagar AND herself when she didn't see the moment of interacting with Hagar as her surrogate as an opportunity to make some demands from Abram, rather than trying to position herself for higher esteem in Abram's eyes (according to Gen. 16:2). Sarai was so busy trying to get Abram to (do what he should have been doing) esteem her, that she ended up attempting to belittle Hagar, asserting the little bit of power that she had as a free woman over Hagar - instead of seeing her as more than just competition. Further, that the entire story is really about Abram and God's promise to him, anyways, really sucks. These two women were just secondary characters in Abrams story. I wish they could have seen themselves as allies rather than enemies.

Isn't that what y'all be doing in the comment section? Vying and fighting for mens attention, approval and esteem in an attempt to be more than a sub-character in the overall plot. So you agree with the archaic, patriarchy poop that they spew and rather than using those opportunities to come together and educate our misguided, privileged brothers on the fact that our body is NOT their party and our worth is greater than what we have on - you add fuel to their fire. *"See, Ayesha agrees with us!"* Further, my point is that sisterhood is likely the answer to so many of our issues. If white feminists would see black women's issues as relevant and important there would be much more power in our fight for equality. That if the Super Saved Sista could see that her judgment does not serve her Twerk Queen Sister they could likely coexist in a world where they honor one another for their choices and MAYBE even influence one another in the areas where they lack. And that if Suzanna could stop seeing Ernestine (who

LACKS a choice and a voice) as a threat and if Sarai could stop seeing Hagar (who LACKS a choice and a voice) as her enemy... then maybe Sarai would have seen it coming that she, also, was just Abrams property. (see Genesis 20 when Abram gives Sarai to Abimelech to keep himself safe. That's why he aint no kind of good).

And this is a side note but we know Father Abraham had some daggon daughters so why does this song only acknowledge your raggely sons?

I digress again.

It goes down in the comment section. And by down I mean literally... it goes DOWN. There is so much negativity and low vibrating insecurity - pandering to menfolk that really need us to join together and say, "Hey. That's dumb. This is how it's gonna be from now on."

In the meantime... I guess... Just don't read the comment section. That's all I got for you right now.

A LOVE LETTER
FROM AN EROTICA GODDESS:
because the body is not an apology
by ebonyjanice

I remember hearing Pearl Cleage speak at a book festival in Decatur, Georgia years ago. Someone asked her how she writes through her writers block. She said, "*Usually I write a letter to whomever it is that is keeping me from being able to tell the truth.*" For me, that person use to be my grandmother before she transitioned into eternity. Now, it is a mix of my Mother and my Aunt Phyllis... and maybe a few other people that I haven't given a name to yet as I process this.

Neither my mother, my aunt, or my grandmother (had ever) have ever said, "Girrrrrl... you can't be over here telling the truth." But, something inside of me is like, "Yo. My family doesn't want the world to know these things about me. Heck... THEY don't want to know these things about me." Nevertheless, I am committed to getting to the truth, telling the truth and being the most authentic version of my truth as possible because... I'm the only one that has to live this life and if I waste this one life of mine trying to be "appropriate" there's only ONE guarantee: I'm NEVER getting another shot at life in this form.

Anyways, back to Pearl. She said that whenever she has a major block she writes a letter to whomever is keeping her from telling the whole truth so I've decided to start there as I open up a bit about sensuality and the erotic being of the body in the black community - specifically the black church (specifically my own body as: The Black Church).

Here are a few things before I move forward:

1. This fear of our sensuality stems from religious ideology that teaches us some really unrealistic truths about our bodies and their purpose.

2. The condemnation that we come under, especially as black women, has been historically constructed as a means of control and degradation.

3. The people that we fear will judge us have their own personal testimony of twerking in a hand stand as well so... Yeah. That part!

*Dear Mother, Aunts, oh... and Uncle Joe... and also Elder Marsha, (cause I don't know that I've ever wanted my Uncle Joe or Elder Marsha to know I'm a freak either...)

Dear All of Yall,

I'm a freak.

Ok. Now that the tape has been ripped off. Get over the sting and let's move forward. Cause this isn't really about you - you just happen to be in the way of me writing this essay and this gots to be dealt with.

(1) This fear of our sensuality stems from religious ideology that teaches us some really unrealistic truths about our bodies and their purpose.

Dear All of Yall,

Haven't you ever been suspicious of Paul's disregard for the natural proclivities of your body? Have you never really sat with the fact that Paul wasn't having any sex at the point that he was writing the texts that we have come to regard as the prominent teachings on 'no sex before marriage?' Paul was single though y'all. Decidedly single. Come on now. We have to humanize Biblical writers because their theology is an extension of their lived experiences and their own un/processed traumas (in addition to the divine inspiration we "believe" inspired their teachings). Paul is the guy that was so passionate about spreading the gospel that he said, "I wish everybody was single like me." (1 Cor.7:7-8). Paul was also the guy that reminded us of his past by calling himself "the chief of sinners." (1 Tim 1:15).

Now, don't get me wrong. I know that Paul calling himself the chief sinner was just leading up to a conversation on how much God had saved him despite his ridiculousness... but I point that out to say people often speak, teach, preach from the places where they have been hurt the most. Is it unreasonable to consider, at all, that Paul was so passionate about singleness and celibacy because he was still healing from how much he had cut the fool prior to his experience with Christ? I don't want to take much time here but let me say this: There are some traumas from my past that STILL have an impact on how I operate, despite the fact that I've been renewed in those areas. For example: I was touched inappropriately as a small girl and that impacted (likely all of) my sexual explorational experiences as a child, likely too young to be experiencing those feelings. As a result of that experience, I am the MOST harsh on all things pertaining to little girls being safe, whole and free. As a result, I spent MANY years teaching and preaching on sexual immorality because THAT is the place where I had been impacted the most and I felt like lingering in text about sexual purity would redeem the "purity" that had been taken from me as a child in some way. I was preaching my story. Is it not possible that Paul was IN THESE STREETS back in the day and did the majority of his teaching from the places he hurt the most; whether all of that teaching was God inspired or personal experience inspired - could we not question Paul's motives at all? Is Paul not human, that we might ask a few more questions about his "why" before we just receive his teaching as the literal and final word?

Whatever. These are not unreasonable questions. But let's move on.

Dear All of Yall,

The fear of our bodies feeling something "other than the holy ghost" has plagued the Christian community, but certainly the African American

Christian community, since forever. We have intimate relationships with phrases like, "Holiness is still right" and we quote Paul, in many ways, more than we quote Christ because Paul is one of our favorite chastisers as it pertains to sin of the flesh. In fact, Christ didn't say a great deal about sex before marriage - (probably) because around the time of Christ girls were married off at around age 12, 13 so there wasn't a great deal of teaching necessary on the topic because -- CHILD MARRIAGE.

You mean to tell me... We still out here scrambling to adhere to the step by step, day by day of a teaching that, for the most part, we recklessly frequent reading out of context. Like... If we're really about this LITERAL translation of the Bible life... Then are we prepared to start marrying our daughters off to their older cousins or the creepy old sheep herder up the street? Cause... I'm just saying. This whole context thing might be important here. Just maybe...

> "Those who live according to the flesh have their minds set on what the flesh desires; but those who live in accordance with the Spirit have their minds set on what the Spirit desires." - Romans 8:5

Dear All of Yall,

Do you ever get sleepy? I do. From time to time. It happens to me every so often. *They Grind I Sleep*. Sometimes *They Sleep I Grind*. Either way... Sleep. It's a thing. That I know of, sleepiness is a natural response of the flesh portion of our self when we need rest. So, errrr, ummm - I'm just wondering if Paul (here he go again) was suggesting that we never acknowledge our bodies at all? Is that our interpretation? Because if so - here's a list of things you need to stop doing NOW and go meditate, pray and levitate instead:

1. Breathe.

2. Eat.

3. Drink.

4. Sleep.

5. Urinate.

6. Defecate.

7. You.

8. Get.

9. The

10. Picture.

"For the flesh desires what is contrary to the Spirit, and the Spirit what is contrary to the flesh. They are in conflict with each other, so that you are not to do whatever you want." - Galatians 5:17

Dear All of Yall,

Let me make something clear - I am, by no means, attempting to argue that the flesh and the spirit aren't two separate entities that often have two different intentions and goals. I am a Freedom Consultant and a Holistic Wellness Coach. As a result of the work that I do around "wholeness", I regularly teach on the importance of paying attention to the 3 Part Man. You exist (in this human form) in your body. You are an eternal spirit. You have a soul. So... When Paul (again) says that the flesh and the spirit are in conflict with one another, while I can agree that the two aren't always on the same mission, I gotta side eye him a little bit because this opposition doesn't necessarily make one evil and one good. I'm sorry, but these 3 parts, while individual entities, go together. It feels a little irresponsible and strategic to teach that they oppose one another when they make up your whole self. [I would not cut out my left eye to exalt my right eye. Together my eyes give me the WHOLE picture. One is not necessarily innately better than the other.] Yes, there are often opposing desires. The spirit (my higher self) longs for eternity while my flesh (my lower self) longs for satisfying pleasure in this present. The idea that these two desires are contrary in an exclusively negative way, however, is a guilt that is taught, socialized and learned. To insist that proving my loftiness in God starts with saying, "I deny my body that God created, gave me (for a reason), strategically designed and knows more intimately than me," is kind of... well, unrealistic. Who told you it was wrong to feel? Who told you it was wrong to feel good? Who told you it was wrong to feel really good? Who told you it was wrong to feel really really good... Ok... You get what I mean? Feeling good can not be categorized as a sin. It appears to be a natural response of the body portion of your "whole" self (Spirit. Soul. Body.) To be clear, God designed the clitoris with all those nerves there for a reason. To insist that responding to the way they naturally lead to arousal is unfair. I could say more here but I know you're still processing the "I'm a freak" part from earlier.

Stick with me though. I'm not here to change your mind about anything. I'm just walking through the text from a liberation perspective. I don't want to encourage anyone to be a slave to their bodies, but I also don't want to encourage anyone to be a slave to ideas that have mostly been taught with no context. Again, context is a thing that matters as we read the text. In fact, it matters a lot.

(2) The condemnation that we come under, especially as black women, has been historically constructed as a means of control and degradation.

Dear All of Yall,

Have you given any thought to the African woman, enslaved in America and everything that she knew to be true before she was stolen, like an object, and brought to a land that, hundreds of years later, still doesn't see her as a whole human? I mean - I know we're walking through a predominately Christian understanding of sensuality but I want to step to the side for a second and say, before Africans were enslaved in America, many (most) had God relationships and spiritual realities that did not include the text that Christians view as the end all be all. So... Consider for a second that prior to the introduction of Christianity to African people, specifically those in America, there were years and years of truth that did not include (what is recognized as) the Christian canon of truth on sensuality, erotica and sexuality. But then Europeans introduced Christ (the homie) to African people in a more aggressive way - and wrestled with (and literally tried to beat) all of the "Africa" (including their religion, the spirituality, their language, their healing practices and their natural expressions of self) out of these people.

Here's the thing though, sexuality was viewed in West Africa so differently from the West that Europeans weren't able to understand, objectively what they were witnessing amongst the African people. They saw sex as "sinful and dirty," while the Africans saw sex as "delightfully human and pleasurable." The idea of sexual repression is largely a European idea. In West African mythology there are many divine beings that relished sexual enjoyment. Yemaya appears full of virtue as a wife but often wild and sensual. Erzulie presents herself seductively demanding total sexual allegiance. Oshun is described as the "embodiment of feminine beauty and grace." The !Kung tribe in West Africa compare sex to food; just as people cannot survive without eating, the !Kung say, hunger for sex can cause people to die.

I know you read all of that and your Christian Demonic Filter (TM)* was beeping on 100 thousand trillion. However, here's the thing about studying religion (specifically Christianity) - stuff existed before your religion existed. Now, by no means am I saying, throw Christ out the window because other stuff existed before him. Please don't. I like Him a lot. However, I am saying that to reject spiritual and religious teachings that make your faith look like the *baby* that it is becomes arrogant; naive at best. I remember when I had the revelation of Judaism being the parent of

Christianity and then Christianity being the older cousin of Islam (the three major monotheistic religions in the world)... I was like, "Why have I been out here acting like there was no kind of God conversation before Moses went up on that mountain? Because there was? There were hundreds and hundreds of YEARS of existence before Moses started writing what we have come to know as some of the most quoted books in the Old Testament. That's important information to consider as you reconcile your faith in the text and the perspective from which the writers wrote the text. You can't just live on "we'll understand it better by and by." Jeremiah prophesied and said that the mysteries would be revealed to those that asked. So that's the proof that God doesn't desire to remain a mystery. Study to show yourself approved. (2 Timothy 2:15). When I was in school, I learned about this thing called "context." I've spoken about context a bit already but I just want to reemphasize the importance of context here: Context is important. Really really important.

So historically, the idea of sensuality has not been a scary thing that any person, married or unmarried, ran from or feared. The fact that the construction of sex as a filthy thing came from someone other than God (Christ specifically) is a problem. You must see it as such in order to really begin to reclaim your body as a naturally responding edifice that alerts you, in this human form, to what you need, when you are hungry, when you are sick, when you are well, when you are in lack... and even when you just wanna zooma zoom zoom and a boom boom... I'm talking bout sex. Zooma zoom... nevermind.

Your body can be a space of healing and wholeness. So why would you continue to deny portions of yourself that are in want? It's not natural and historically your people have NEVER deemed hormones as a thing to reject or hide from. That the body is a thing that you should apologize* for is such an obnoxious idea that I legitimately feel irritated thinking about how long I allowed myself to be in bondage about basic things like: self exploration, masturbation, balancing my sacral chakra... shoot - keeping my mother freaking chakras open to begin with! Why did it take me so long to get free?

bell hooks says that in many instances the fascination and subsequent fear of black sexuality is just another example of the ways that the bodies of black folk are used to serve the interest of the system that has no intentions of fostering or promoting the growth or freedom of those people. I want to go into the idea of black bodies as property, rape of enslaved women by white slave masters and overseers, breeding during slavery, the statistics of brown skinned women and girls being sold into sex slavery today and the whorophobia of any black woman that chooses sexual liberation over socially constructed ideas of "modesty" -- but I still have more to say and this *Love Letter* is getting long. Just know that historically white supremacy has profited greatly off of telling you what to do and what not to do with your body. So... Context. Again. Knowing the WHOLE story is a thing that matters.

There is so much to say about this - but the last thing I'll say on this topic is back to the African woman... I was thinking about Hagar (because I'm always thinking about Hagar) and how we all learned the story of Father Abraham as a small girl and nobody (not even me) ever spent any time dealing with Hagar's sexual agency being stolen from her. If we are to understand this story from the Christian perspective, we realize that Sarai offered Hagar to Abram as a concubine and a surrogate since she could not get pregnant on her own. I've blogged about this and Facebook'd about this, essayed about this and talked and lamented and grieved about this... that Hagar was raped. But the gotcha gotcha is - how easily we glossed over that piece in church. It did not matter that Hagar was raped. The rapist and the sex trafficker somehow become the heroes of this story.

This young Egyptian girl had no say over her body and ended up giving birth to a child that would later become a bastard. Here's the problem... Sarai, operating in patriarchal constructs that would soon misuse her as well, (1) gave Hagar to Abram (2) then felt jealous that Hagar got pregnant (3) then caused Abram to reject Hagar and his child because she was in her feelings. How often have black bodies been the source of LIFE and then shamed for being able to actualize in magnificently divine ways? Is it possible that in the same ways that Europeans misused scripture to enslave Africans they also misused the text to vilify the body; specifically the black body? Is it simply ironic that Hagar, an African slave, had her sexual agency stolen from her through the system of slavery and now here we are "free" but still allowing our sexual agency to be stolen; only functioning freely with the permission of a system outside of our own selves? And is it possible that being such a sexually repressed people has even disconnected us from the divine? That is certainly a discussion all by itself... but I'm saying.

These are not unreasonable questions. But let's move on.

(3) The people that we fear will judge us have their own personal testimony of twerking in a hand stand as well so... Yeah. That part!

Dear All of Yall,

I'm not here to put any of y'alls individual business in the streets. I wouldn't even presume to know details and specifics about your sheets (former or current). BUT... I'mma just ask these few little questions and I'mma get out your way:

(1) Have you ever had sex?
(a) Before marriage? (b) With more than one person?

(2) Have you ever done miscellaneous other activities with a person other than yourself or your imagination?

(3) Wasn't it amazing?

(4) Did you feel guilty afterwards?

(5) If so... Was that guilt your own? Or did you have to remember that you weren't supposed to enjoy those miscellaneous activities?

When I was attempting to work up the nerves to write this letter to you all, confessing that I'm basically an erotica goddess*, I had some conversations with some sister friends in a private group on Facebook. One of them said, (brace yourself it's crude): "I'm sure whoever you're fearing judgement from has seen a penis or two in their life." Actually... That's inauthentic. She said, "I'm sure whoever you're fearing judgement from has licked and sucked on a penis or two in their life."

(covers mouth and giggles)

I thought to myself, "You know whaaaaaaaaat? They have! Pretty much all of y'all in my "All of Yall" have had some sex. Maybe more than one sex. Maybe even a LOT of sex. Possibly even multiple sexes. And you know why you had more than one sex? Because you liked it. In fact, you liked it a lot. And if you're honest, you wish you would have walked through much of this conversation YEARS ago when you were living in condemnation over something that felt so natural to you. But nooooooo... You couldn't be honest with yourself or those preaching and teaching the gospel of "save it for marriage" when most of your Sunday School teachers have seen and touched more than one penis in their life as well... I mean... Keep it real bruh! Those old ladies didn't have 12 children and 2 or 3 different baby daddy's on accident. So whaaaaat is all this shaming we keep on doing of one another for?

Listen... I don't have all the answers. I am "becoming" still. But as I am "becoming" I am realizing that much of what use to be the absolute truth to me is hazy. I have had sex. Quite a bit of sex. I enjoyed it very much. (insert Bird Man hand rub and creepy old man grin here). At print, I am 33 years old. I am unmarried. I'm not currently having sex right now but if I can keep it trill (and I will cause this is my book and I'm grown) I'm probably only not having sex because I don't have a man (it happens to be my preference to be in an exclusive relationship before I put my hands up on my hips I dip, you dip, we dip). If I was in a committed relationship right now, however, I probably would be P-popping in a handstand right now off the end of a bed instead of writing this blog... But I don't. So here I am - celibate than a mug. Consciously and unashamedly.

There may be judgment for that truth but I'm keeping it real. What I do know is that, unprovoked, my body makes requests. If I am hungry - I eat food to satisfy that craving. If I am thirsty - I drink so that I can stop being thirsty. If I feel horny - I... (turns around, touches the ground, gets back up, works it on down).

Dear All of Yall,

I'm sorry. But current theology is often incomplete in that it fails to deal with the erotic realities and relationships that comprise the complex expressions of human fulfillment. Basically... while I came here to just confess that I'm a freak so I could get free from the judgment that you may or may not have for me... I ultimately just want to end by reinforcing the fact that the body has noooo reason to apologize. I hope you don't ever apologize for what 1/3 of your whole self needs when it needs what it needs. And I hope you don't ever apologize for the times when all you wanna do is zooma zoom zoom zoom and a boom boom.

So many words.
So little time.

Sinceriously,

EbonyJanice of The Free People Project

(*) Christian Demonic Filter (TM) - I started calling the gauge I used to determine if something was "demonic" (defined as not Christian/not in the Bible/Jesus didn't say this/too much spirit and not enough holy/or sometimes, actually demonic like a demon) - my Christian Demonic Filter (TM).

(*) The body is not an apology is a phrase that I got from my sister friend, Sonya Renee, on unapologetic radical self love.

(*) What is an Erotica Goddess. (creepy grin) You're too young to know. Maybe I'll define this for you later. But you gotta grow up a little first.

Time for Some Action:
On Activism and
Why It Ought to be Intersectional
by Nikki Blak

I once wrote that to be black is to be both invisible and conspicuous all at once. This is an experience that I've lived, yes even in sweet little post racial America. Yes, even in a "melting pot" such as Los Angeles and in an extremely left state such as sunny California. I have felt as though people have looked right through me about as frequently as I've felt I was being gawked at. And maybe the behaviors of the individuals that have been overly conscious of my whereabouts in a room and proximity to them at all times and the behavior of the ones that have completely ignored me was totally benign and a byproduct of being socially awkward, disconnected from humans in these modern times, or just generally rude and lacking proper home training. But here's the thing... As a black person, you always have to wonder if these behaviors are a reaction to your color.

That's the key to white privilege. The privilege doesn't lie in what you *do* have but instead, what you *don't* have. You don't have to be paranoid about whether or not people's reactions to you have anything to do with your race. You don't have to wonder if you're going to step into the local general supply store and be able to find products for your hair or a doll that is the same color as your child. You don't have to have knowledge of or care about anyone else's history, culture or traditions. You don't have to see color. You don't even have to be in possession of race yourself, as you're the default. Just based on these examples alone, we can see that a lot of being white is *not doing*. There's no activity necessary. Therefore, one could reason that in the inverse, being a person of color *is* about doing. Being black is being burdened with activity, whether emotional, cerebral, or physical. And in the same way that being white is about not exerting yourself, benefiting from white privilege and giving permission to individuals, institutions and practices that perpetuate bias, inequality and oppression and therefore being complicit in civil rights and human rights violations that happen as a result of systemic racism is fueled by inactivity. If every white person simply sits idly by and spectates as racism persists, then Global White Supremacy will likely reign unchallenged, forever. The fact that I even have to pontificate about these things, yet alone type them is nothing short of exhausting.

Being a black woman in America wears me out. I literally wake up every morning tired, still burdened by the white folk shenanigans of the day (and centuries) before and in constant anticipation of new mayonnaise infused foolery that will inevitably blossom like a disgusting colonization scented flower and reveal itself more and more with each bullet discharged from a cop's gun into an unarmed black body, every utterance spewing from Rush Limbaugh's mouth and every ages old black hairstyle that popular culture suddenly discovers and appropriates. I tell you, I am worn down into the ground. I can't even imagine how my ancestors must have felt if I, living in relative freedom am weary.

Alas, brother James Baldwin said, "To be a negro in this country and to be relatively conscious is to be in a rage almost all the time." I feel that. Then I wonder, what is it to be woman on this Earth and to be relatively conscious? I can honestly say that I don't even have language to describe it, but one thing is for sure – I don't know what to do with my hands. So then, how does it feel to be both black and woman and be conscious? I'll tell you, it is a wonder that I am in my right mind and able to function at all in society. Actually, many of us aren't. One has to wonder if it is the constant siege on our individual and collective psyches and the ongoing dehumanization that the world at large practices in constant attacks on blackness that is responsible for much of our lack of emotional and mental wellness.

Enter, discussions about mental health. Also, enter conversation about spirituality and what role that plays. Traditionally, as a community, black people have been irresolute about seeking professional psychological help in the form of therapy and instead relied heavily on religion and the Bible. I would venture to say that in most cases, this tendency to lean on the Lord and address emotional and mental instability with The Good Book has been a practice completely detached from spirituality. Meditation and self actualization are customarily frowned upon, but prayer and belief in miracles is encouraged. Sadly, it seems that the black church picks and chooses which mystical phenomena it will give credence to, while often completely disregarding applied sciences, such as psychology.

James 2:14-26 issues a challenge to the brand of thinking that promotes passiveness and reliance on outside entities and factors to right life's wrongs. "What *does it* profit, my brethren, if someone says he has faith but does not have works? Can faith save him? If a brother or sister is naked and destitute of daily food, and one of you says to them, 'Depart in peace, be warmed and filled,' but you do not give them the things which are needed for the body, what *does it* profit? Thus also faith by itself, if it does not have works, is dead."

Enter, activism. It is not enough to simply exist in this world and not contribute to it in a way that affects positive change. It is a basic requirement of humanity. As people, it is our duty and it is not negotiable. As spiritual people, religious people, enlightened people, members of Christ's body – however it is that you identify, it is your duty as a human being on the planet Earth to show up right and in a big way. It is not negotiable. Because, to exist in silence is to be complicit in acts of violence committed against our brothers and sisters. And by "brothers and sisters" I don't mean people that look, think, speak, act, and believe like you. Because our desire for liberation and our acts to further that cause must be intersectional, or else it is of no use at all.

On the back end, activism that is intersectional is beneficial because it increases the likelihood that you will have allies willing to rise up on your behalf when you're in need of wrestling an oppressive boot off of and away from your neck. However, in the short term, intersectional activism is beneficial to those that participate in it because it is who we as decent, peace and justice loving humans are called to be. It is when we are challenging systems of oppression that we are showing up in the fullness of our humanity. This fullness is a manifestation of the all knowing, dynamic spirit and architect of the universe that some of us identify as God. When I am acting on behalf of others (and by extension, myself) I am recognizing and embodying the creator by engineering and orchestrating change.

It is through my intersectional activism that I am made more visible. It is through my spirituality, one that is not faith filled but lacking in works, one that grants me permission to act on my own behalf and that of others, one that urges me to be healthy and balanced in mind and body, that I am made more visible. This visibility that I speak of is not one that serves to bolster my own ego or make me appear wise or important in my own eyes or the eyes of others. It is a visibility that gives others permission to embody grace, demand justice for all people and live in freedom as agents of change. It is a visibility that awakens those among us that are not yet conscious and informs those among us that desire to model world citizenship as a member of the human family that cares and is concerned about the liberties and well being of others. It is a visibility that provides the foundation on which to build community. It is a visibility that empowers and provides hope.

There isn't a doubt in my mind that I am living my ancestors' wildest dreams. I have relative freedom. I am acknowledged as a full person and citizen of the United States of America, at least on paper. I have the ability to read and the right to vote. There is hope for me. So despite being weary as a result of constant confrontations with cis-hetero-patriarchy and global white supremacy, I have hope. And whether I'm aware of it or not, I'm inspiring hope in someone else. That knowledge does not quell the smoldering rage or purge the ache from my tired bones. But it motivates me out of bed each morning and compels me to choose peace in my pursuit of visibility and equality, as I live the experience of being both black and female.

References

Badu, Erykah. Mama's Gun. Erykah Badu. Motown, 2000. CD.

Badu, Erykah. New Amerykah. Erykah Badu. Universal Motown Records, 2007. CD.

Beyonce. Formation. Mike Will Made It, Beyonce, A+, 2016. CD.

Duran, Jane. "Women Of The Civil Rights Movement: Black Feminism And Social Progress." Philosophia Africana 17.2 (2015): 65-73. Academic Search Complete. Web.

Hamblin, J. (2016, June 16). Toxic Masculinity and Murder. Retrieved from http://www.theatlantic.com/health/archive/2016/06/toxic-masculinity-and-mass-murder/486983/

hooks, bell. Ain't I a Woman: Black Women and Feminism. Boston, MA: South End Press, 1981. Print.

Kruger, Daniel J., Maryanne L. Fisher, and Paula Wright. "Patriarchy, Male Competition, And Excess Male Mortality." Evolutionary Behavioral Sciences8.1 (2014): 3-11. PsycARTICLES. Web.

Larrieux, Amel. Bravebird. Amel Larrieux, Laru Larrieux, Threadhead, Basho Ink. Blisslife, 2003. CD.

Marcotte, A. (2016, June 13). Overcompensation Nation: It's time to admit that toxic masculinity drives gun violence.

Retrieved from http://www.salon.com/2016/06/13/
overcompensation_nation_its_time_to_admit_that_toxic_masculinit
y_drives_gun_violence/

Messner, MICHAEL A. Politics of Masculinities Men in Movements.
Sage Publications, 1997. Web.

Mitchell, Donald, Jr., et al. *Intersectionality Higher Education :
Theory, Research, Praxis*. n.p.: New York, New York : Peter Lang,
2014., 2014. *Ashford University Library Ebook Collection*. Web.

Mohl, Allan S. "Monotheism: Its Influence On Patriarchy And
Misogyny." *The Journal Of Psychohistory* 43.1 (2015): 2-20.
PsycINFO. Web.

Roberts, Dorothy. "Reproductive Justice, Not Just Rights." *Dissent
(00123846)* 62.4 (2015): 79-82. *Academic Search Complete*. Web.

Solange. A Seat at the Table. Solange. Saint Records/Columbia,
2016. CD.

Sullivan, Shannon. Revealing Whiteness. [Electronic Resource] :
The Unconscious Habits Of Racial Privilege. n.p.: Bloomington :
Indiana University Press, c2006., 2006. Ashford University Library
Ebook Collection. Web.

Walker, Alice. The Color Purple. London: Women's Press, 1992.
Print.

Watkins, V. (2016). Contested Memories: A Critical Analysis of the Black Feminist Revisionist History Project. Journal Of Pan African Studies, 9(4), 271-288.

Young, Thelathia N., and Shannon J. Miller. "Asé." *Journal Of Religious Ethics* 43.2 (2015): 289-316. *Academic Search Complete.* Web.

Nikki Blak is a poet, public speaker, radical womanist, sociologist, critical race theorist, bottled water connoisseur, and swears up and down she's been parenting poorly since 1999.

ebonyjanice is a scholar, activist, preacher, teacher, coach, hip hop womanist, and double dutch champion. She has never won a double dutch championship but all that other stuff is the truth.

Made in the USA
Coppell, TX
10 June 2020